Fairies and Mermaids
COLORING BOOK

BASED ON PAINTINGS BY
TIFFANY TOLAND-SCOTT

a Tito

publication

Fairies and Mermaids
COLORING BOOK

28 images, and 2 copies of each included!

This book is designed to be colored primarily with dry media, but if you want to use markers, just make sure to put a piece of paper between the pages to prevent bleed-through.

This book is all yours! Feel free to remove pages or dismantle the book, as you wish!

If you'd like to buy a digital copy that you can download and print out on your preferred paper, just visit www.titoland.com/books-and-calendars to view all downloadable coloring book options!

See more art at www.titoland.com

Fairies and Mermaids Coloring Book
by Tiffany Toland-Scott
First Published June 2016
Published by TitoLand
ISBN: 978-0692730850

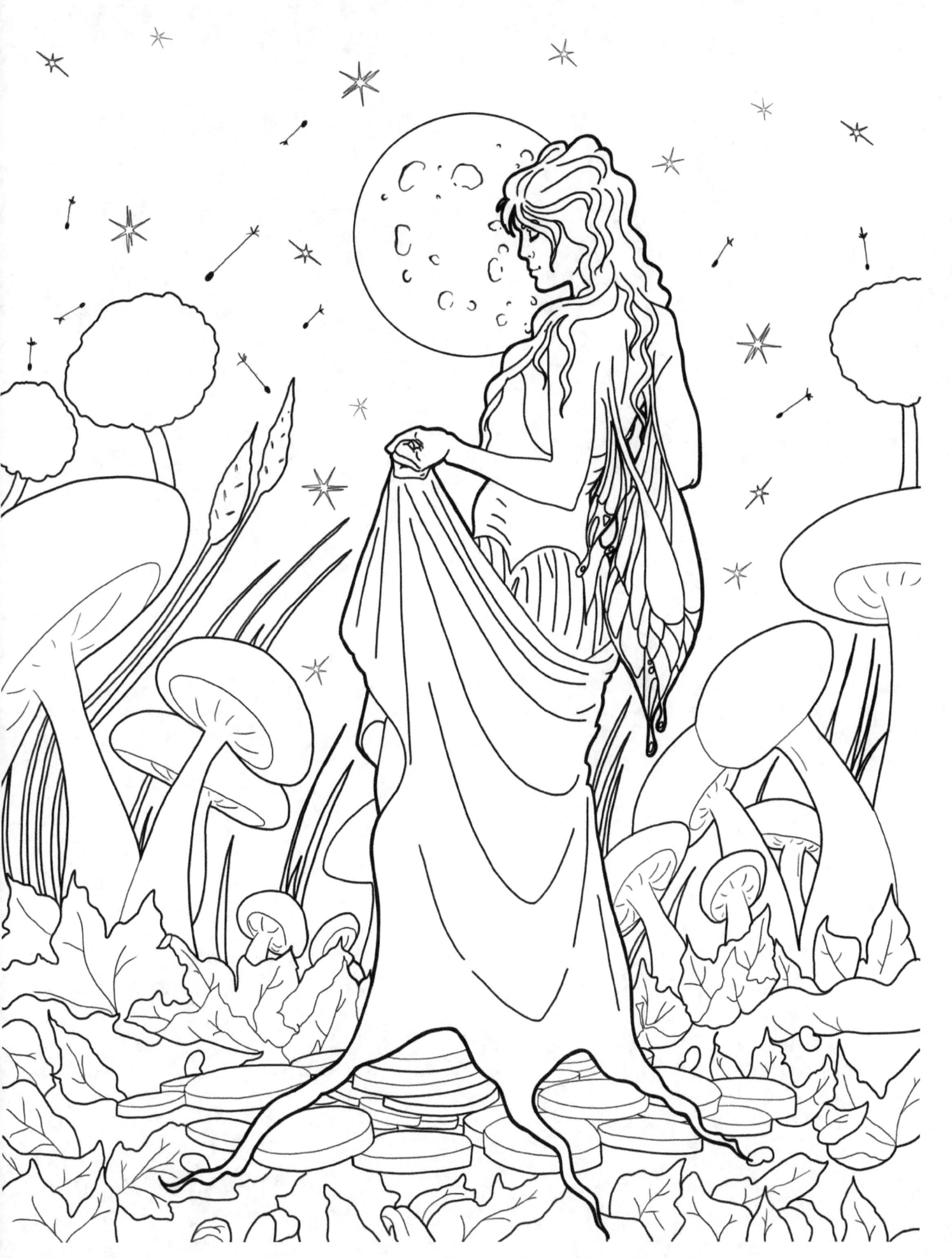

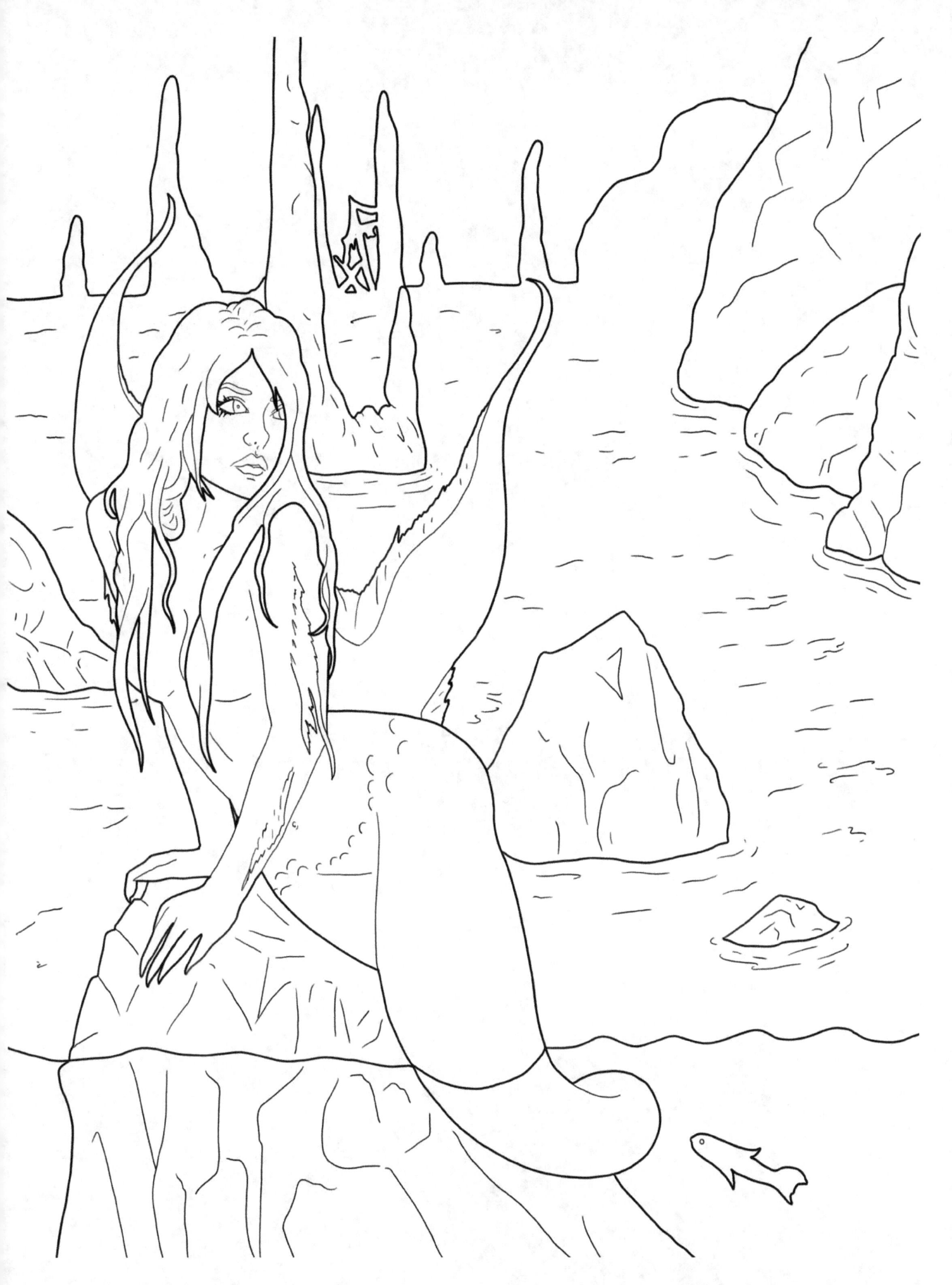

"SIREN'S SONG"

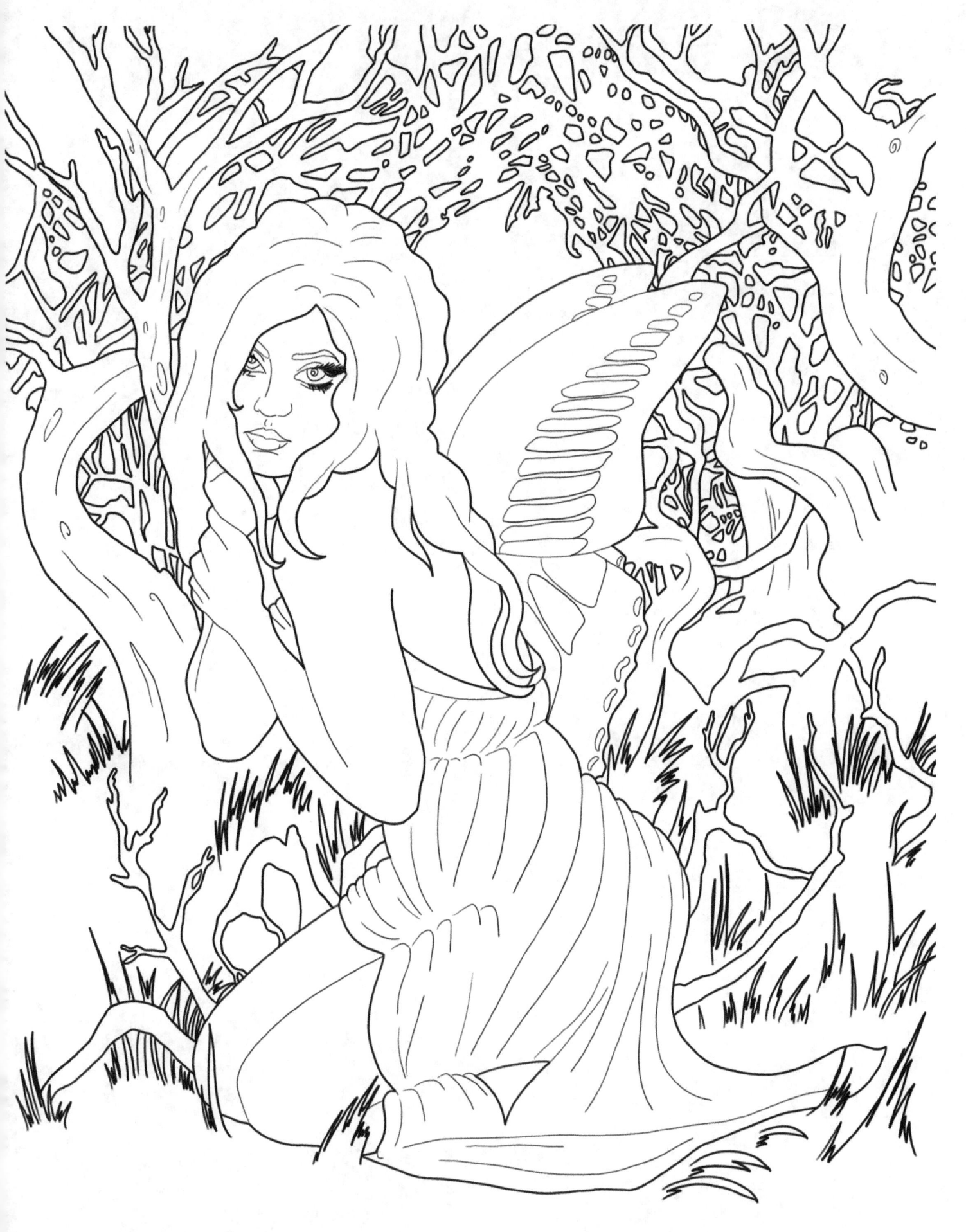

"BLUEBOTTLE"

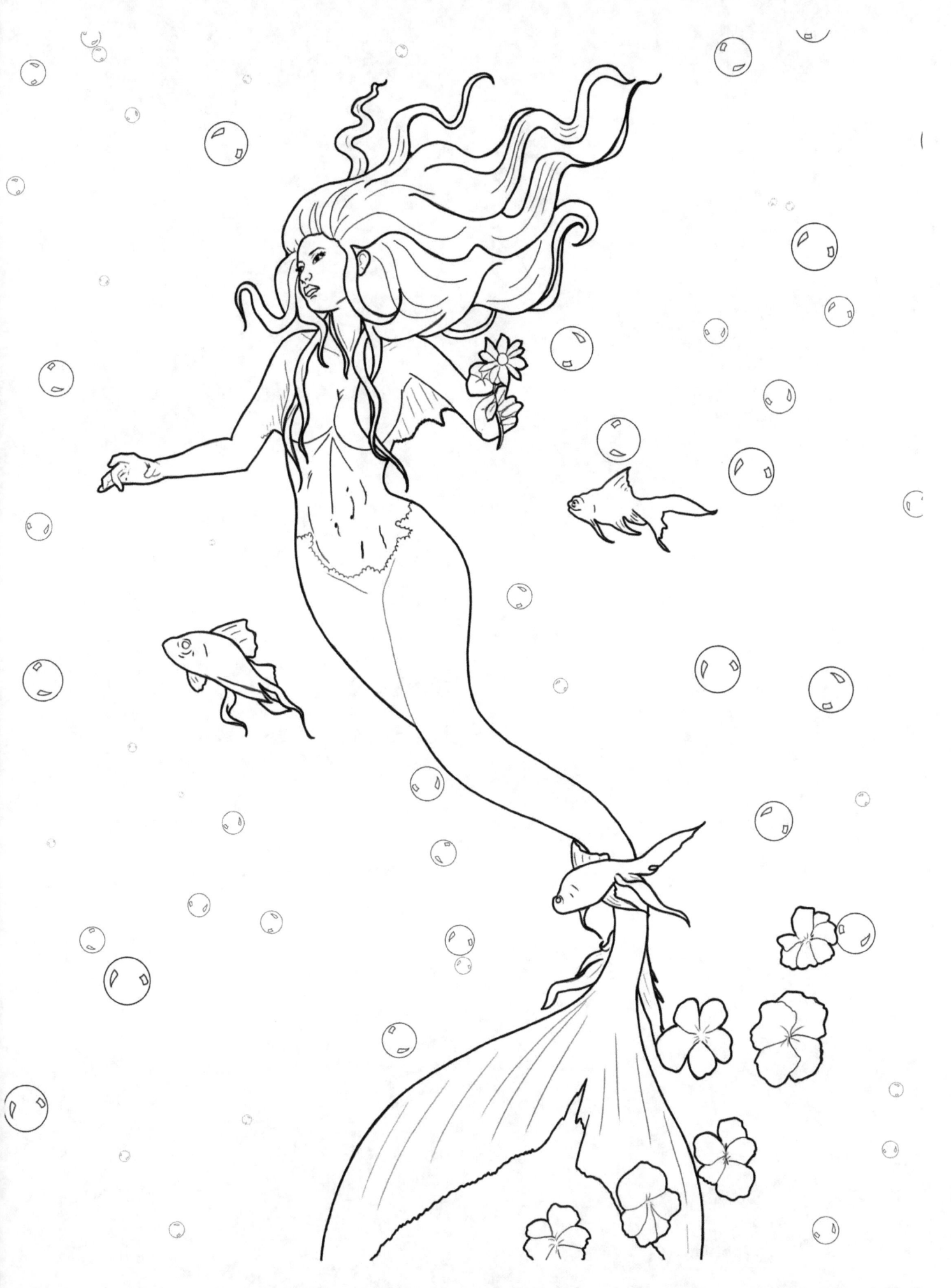

"FORBIDDEN DESIRE"

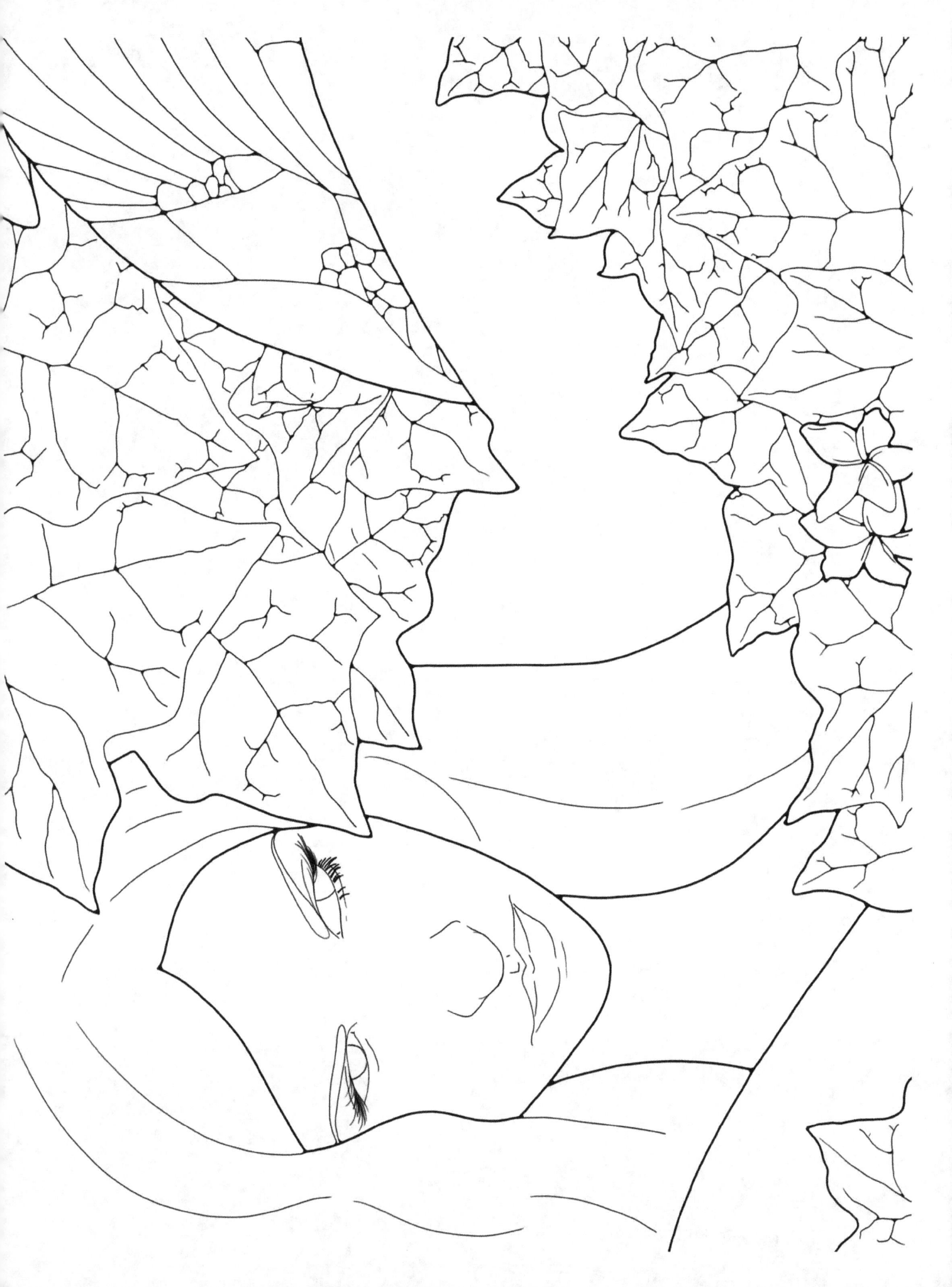

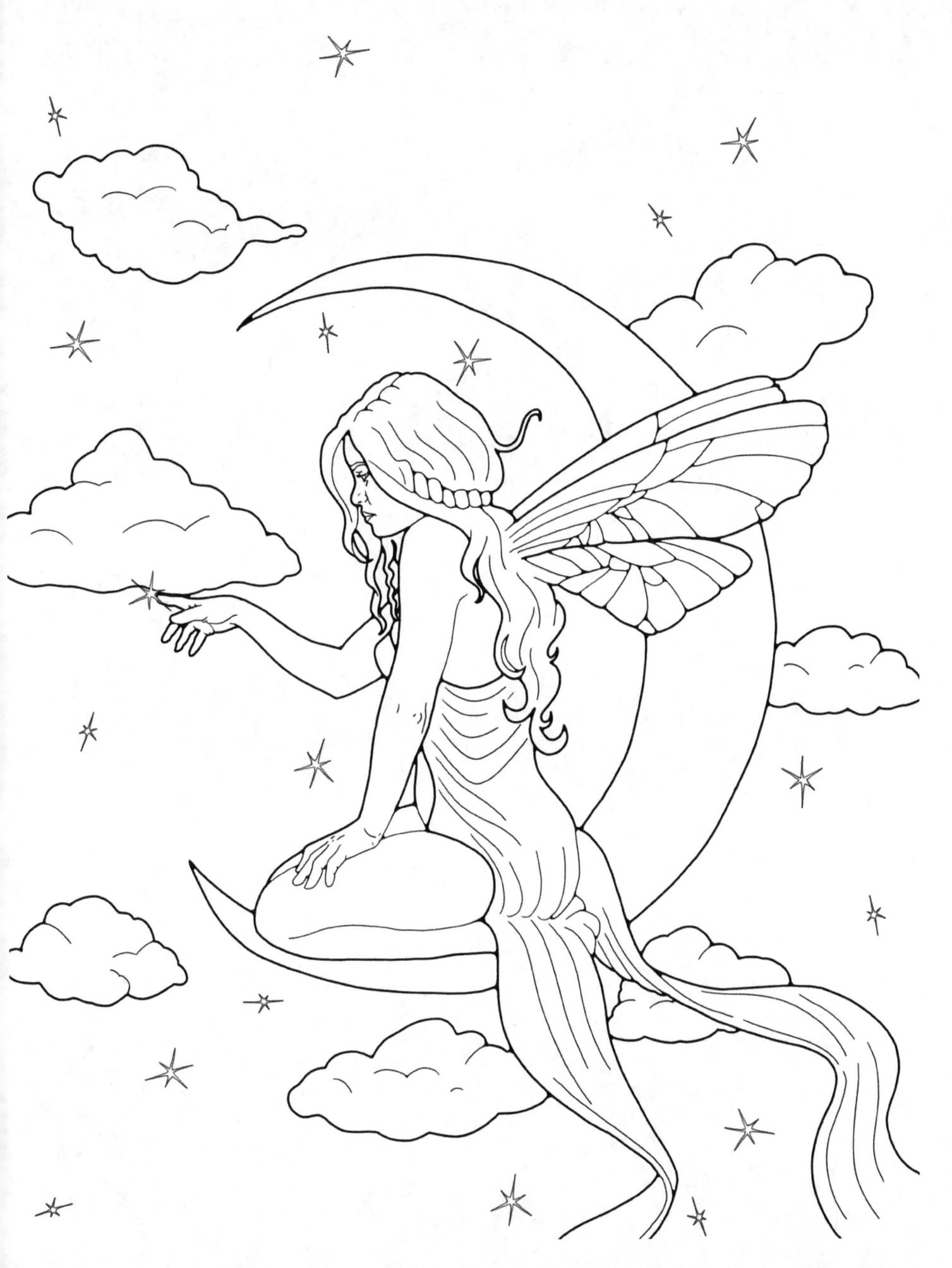

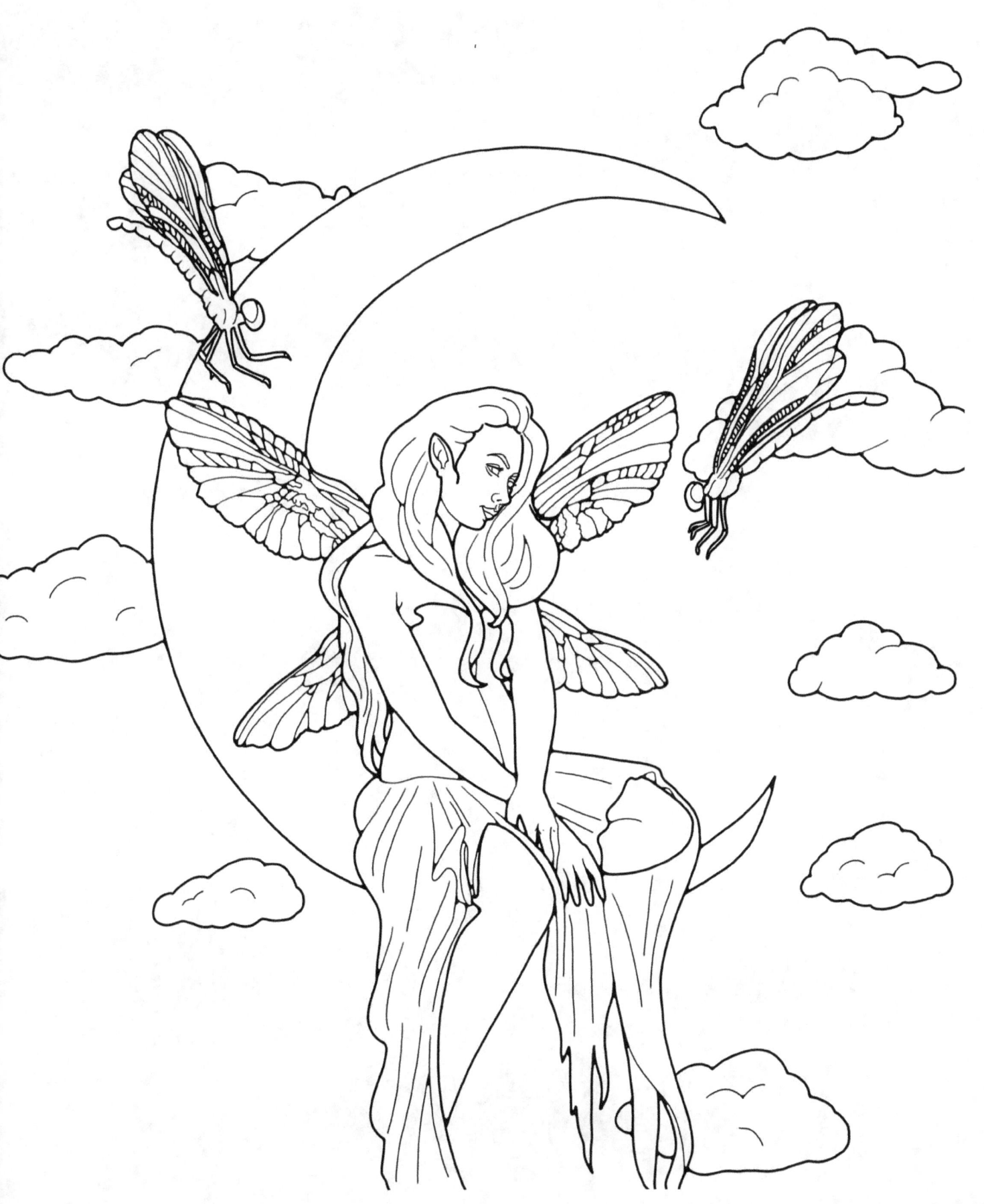

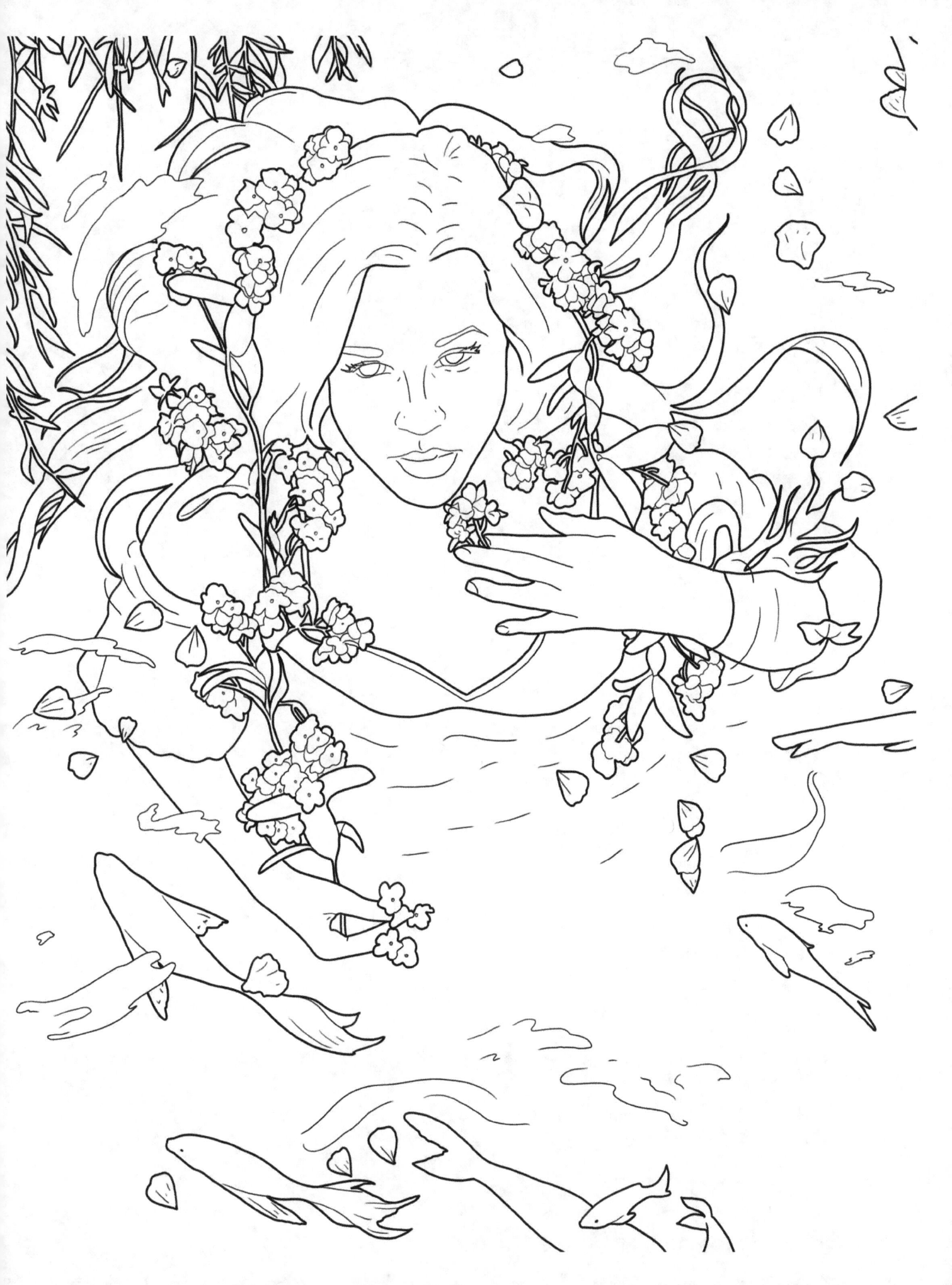

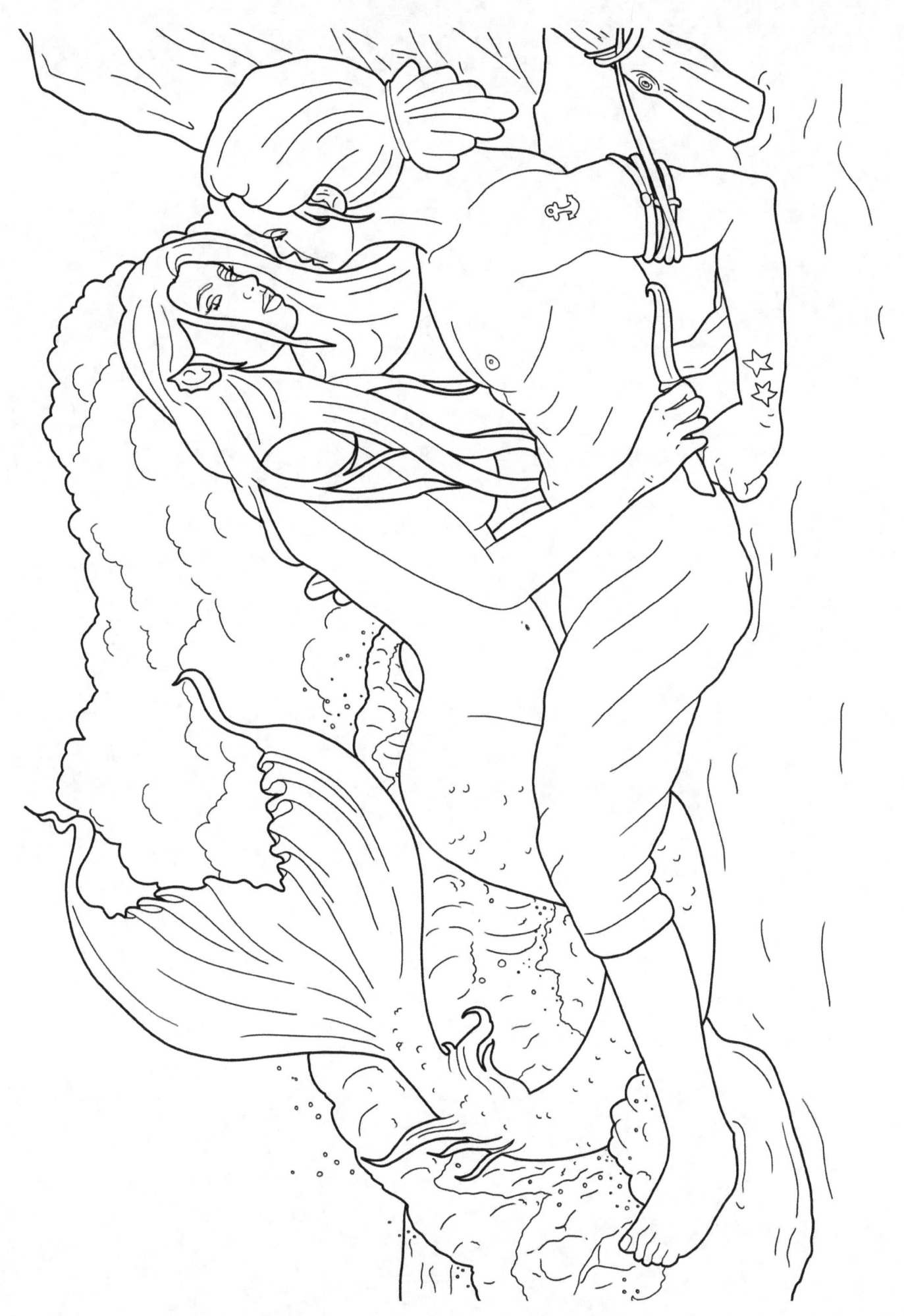

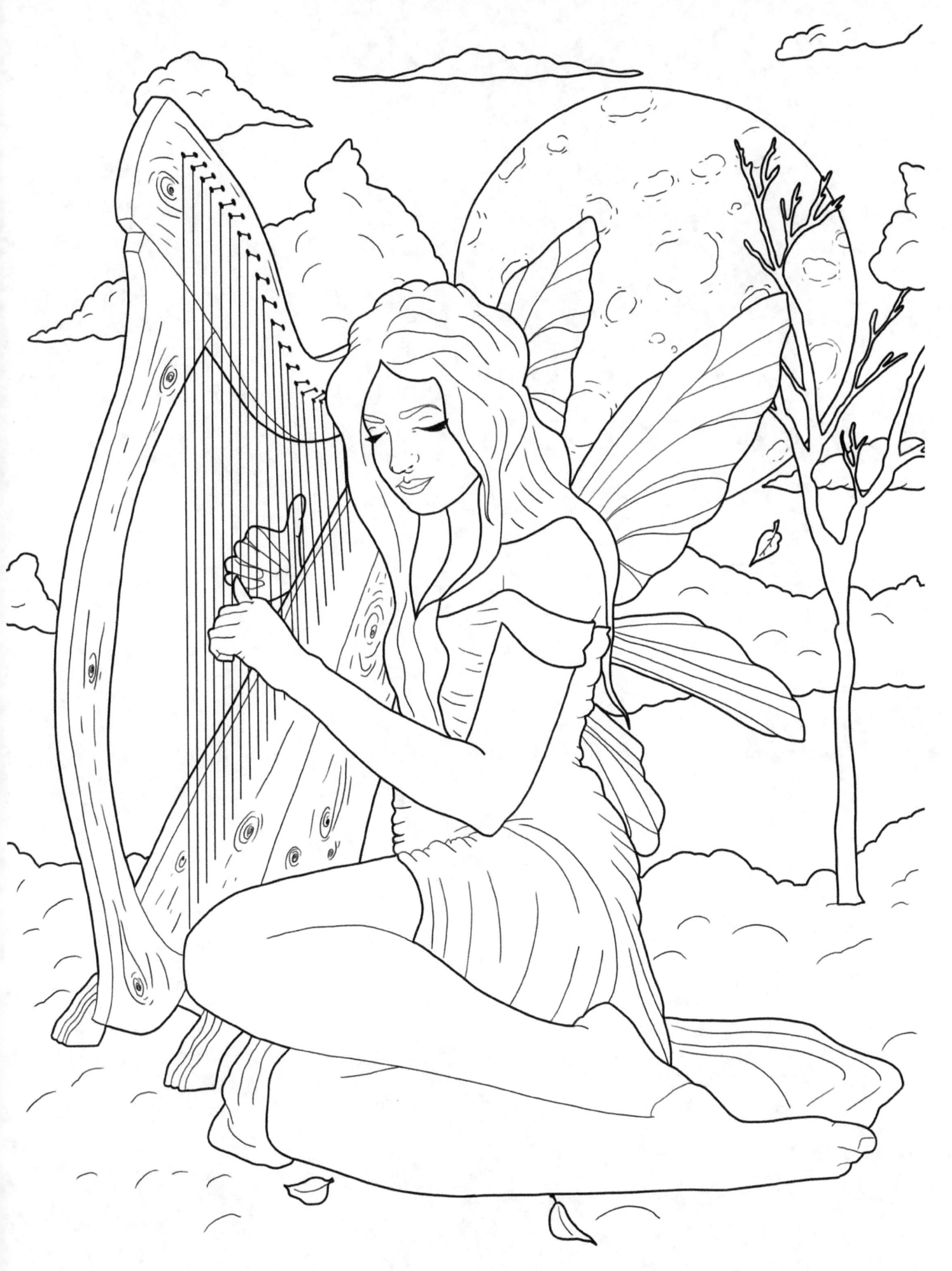

"BEYOND TIME"

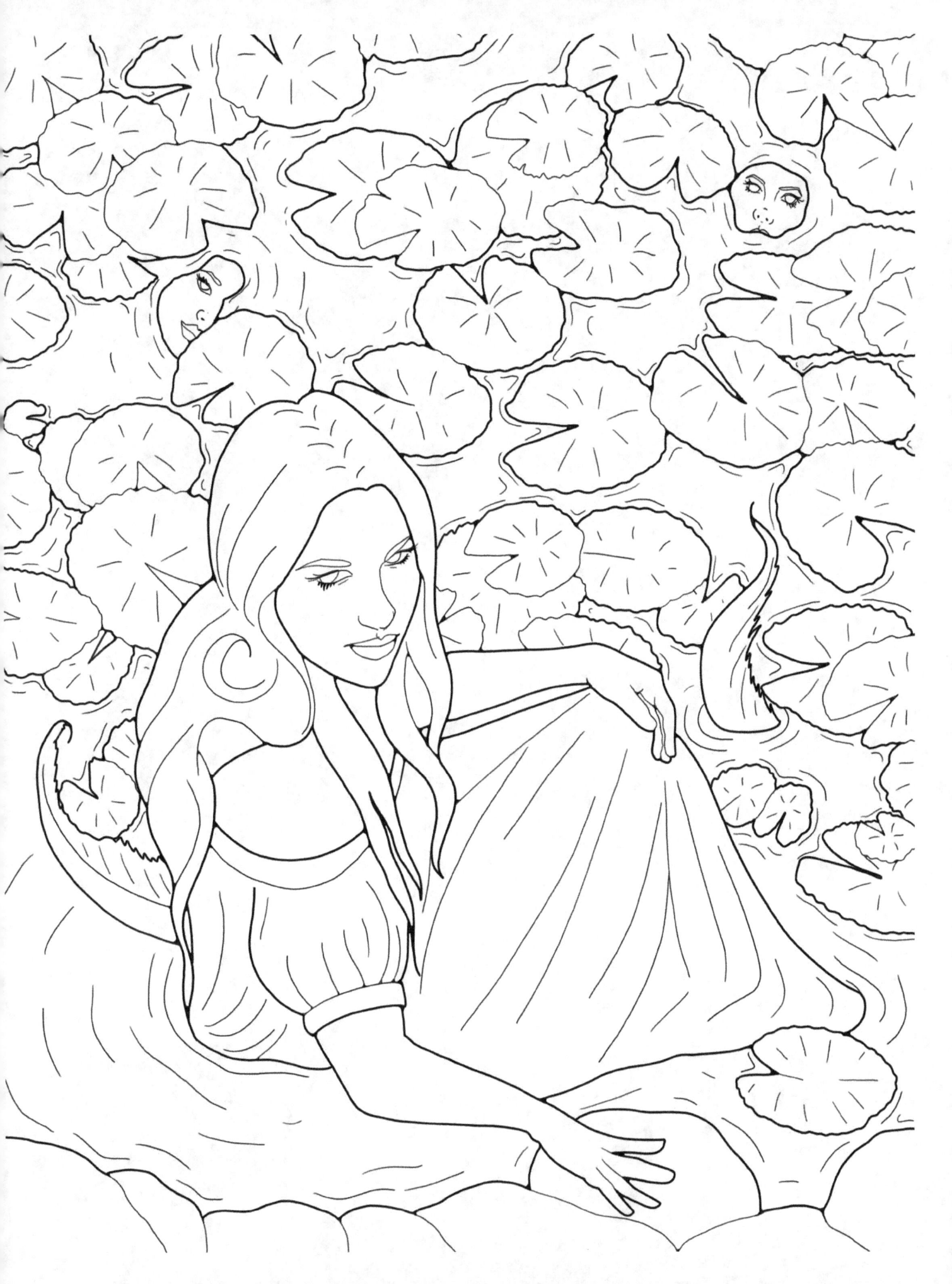

"JOIN US?"

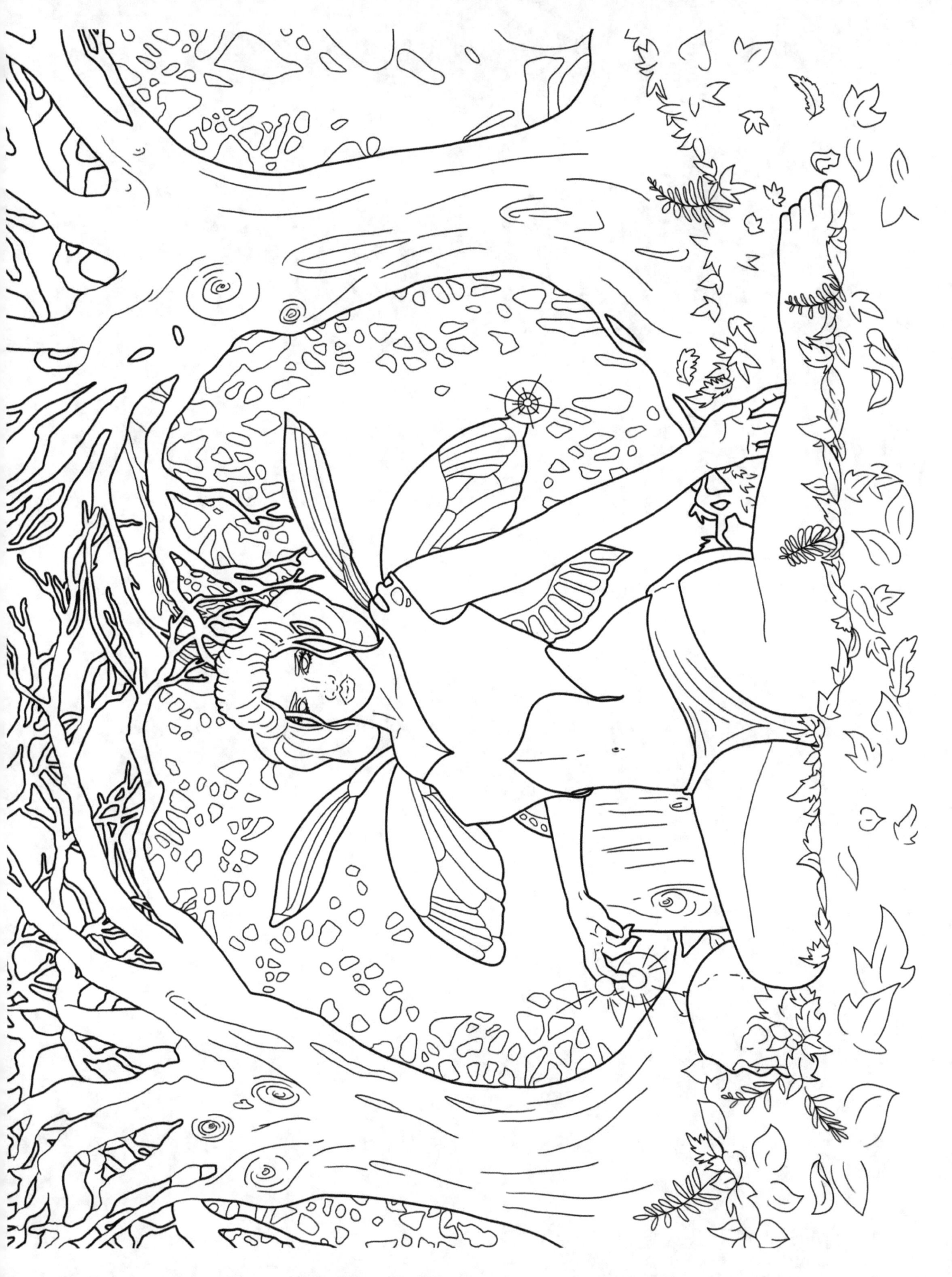

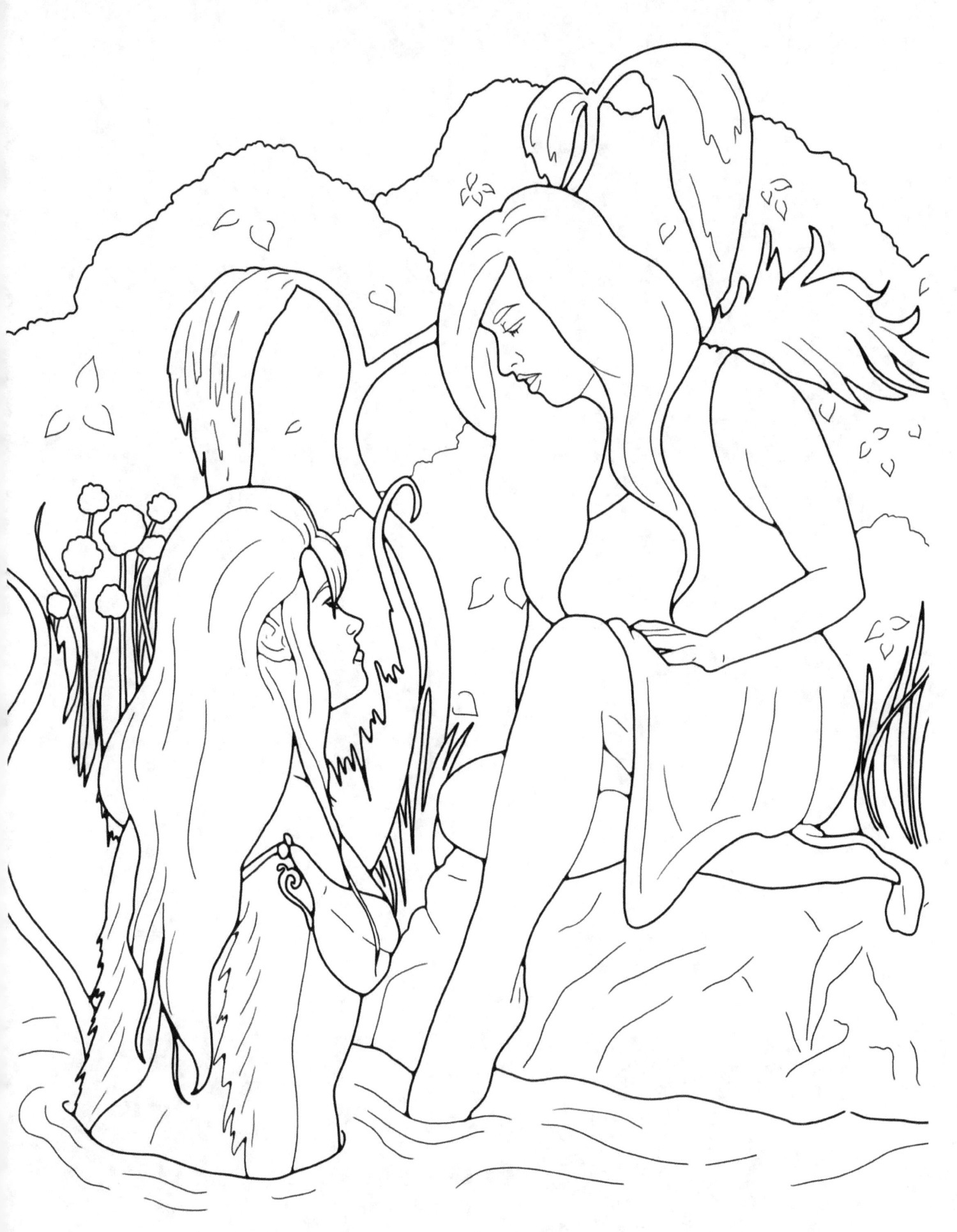

"WORLDS APART"

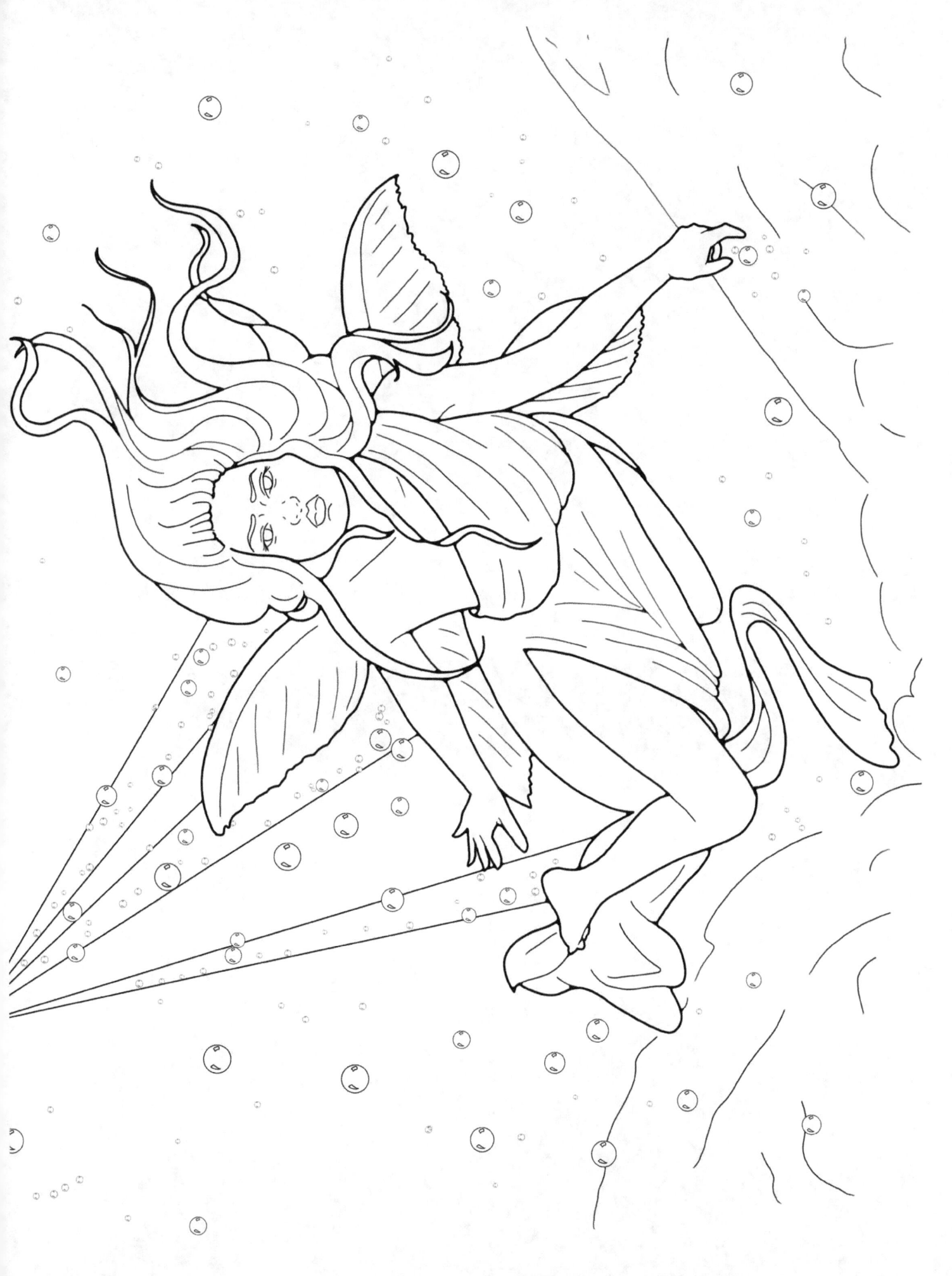

"MELUSINE"

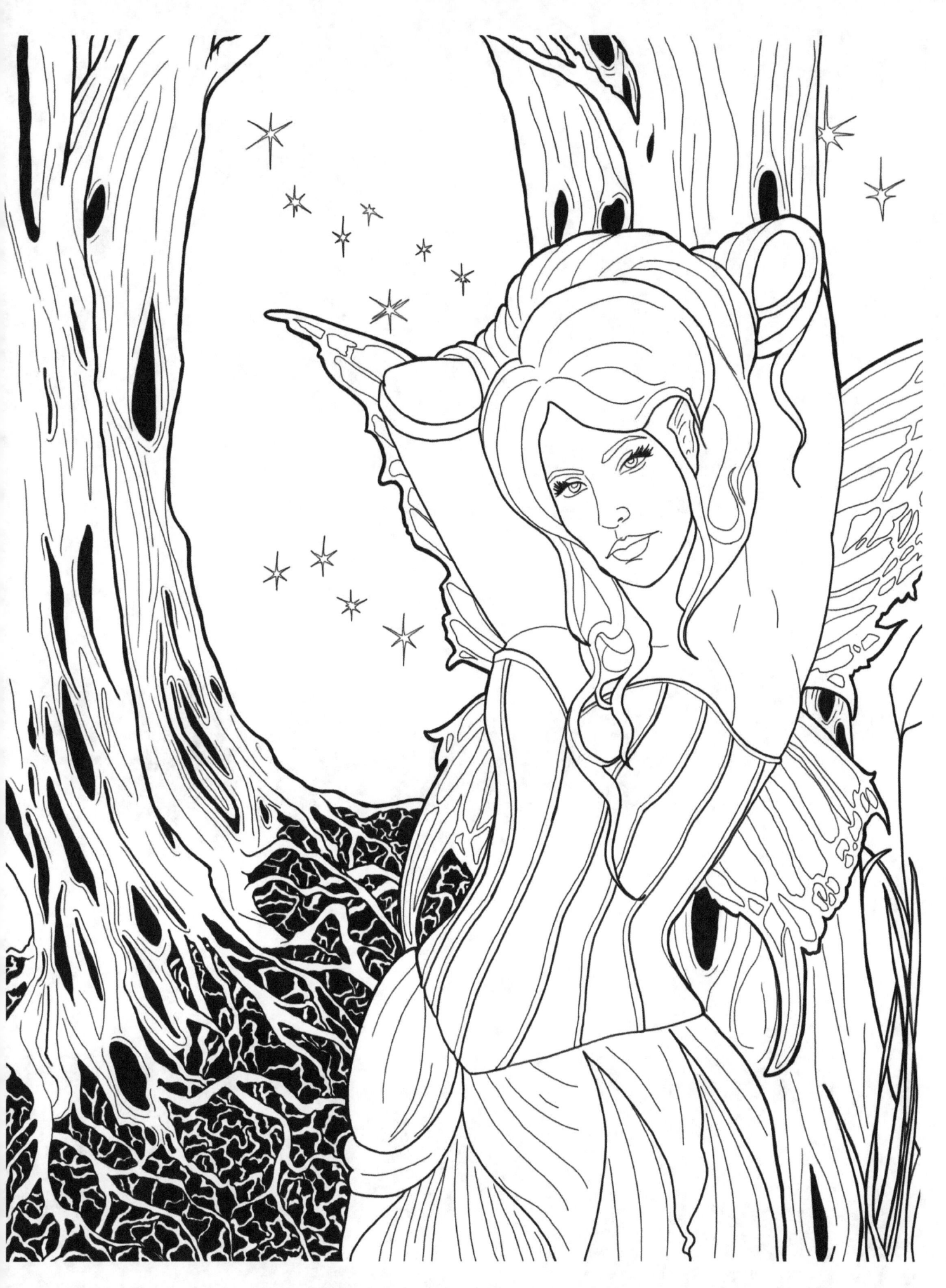

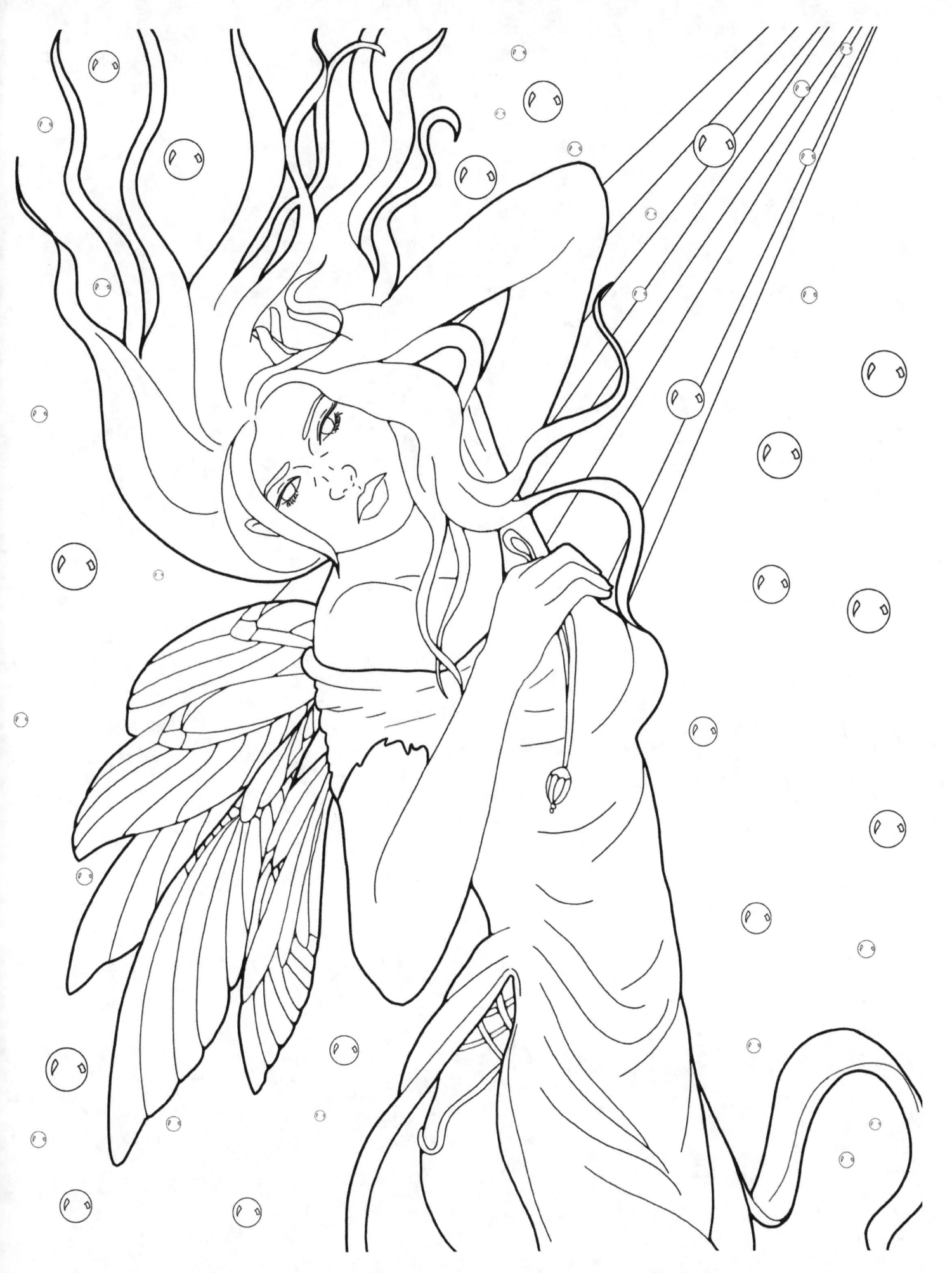

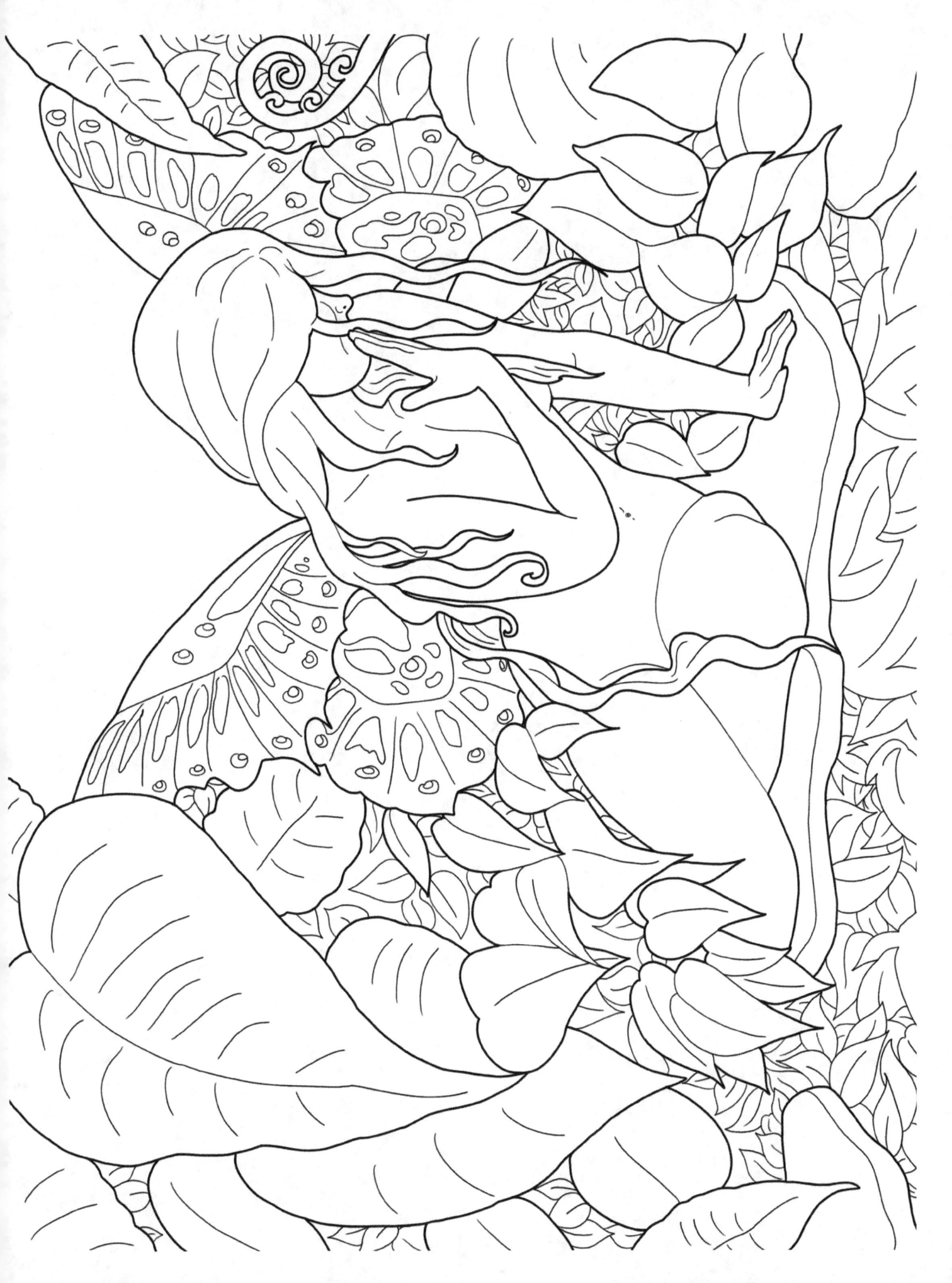

"SHY"

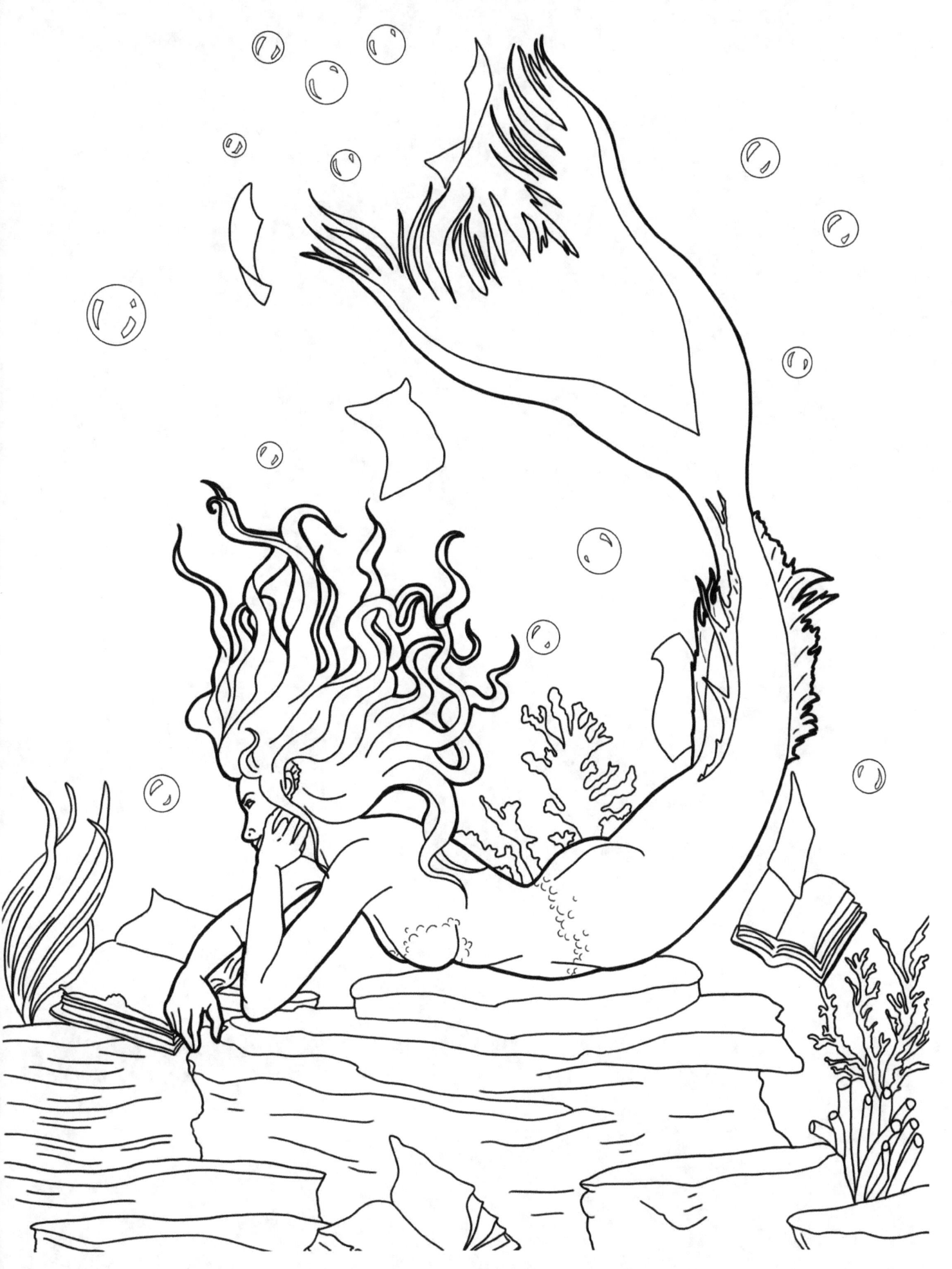

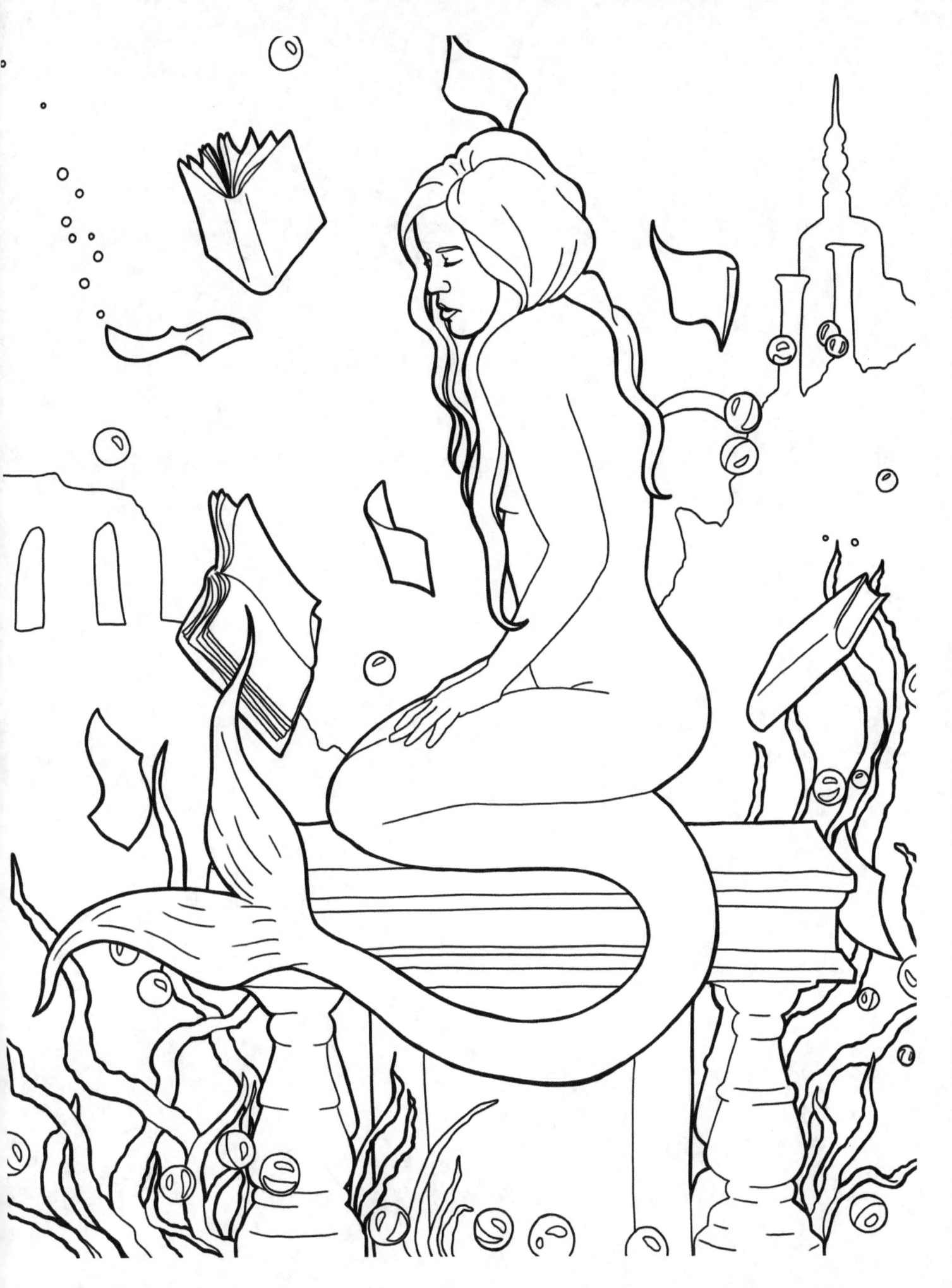

"LOST BOOKS II"

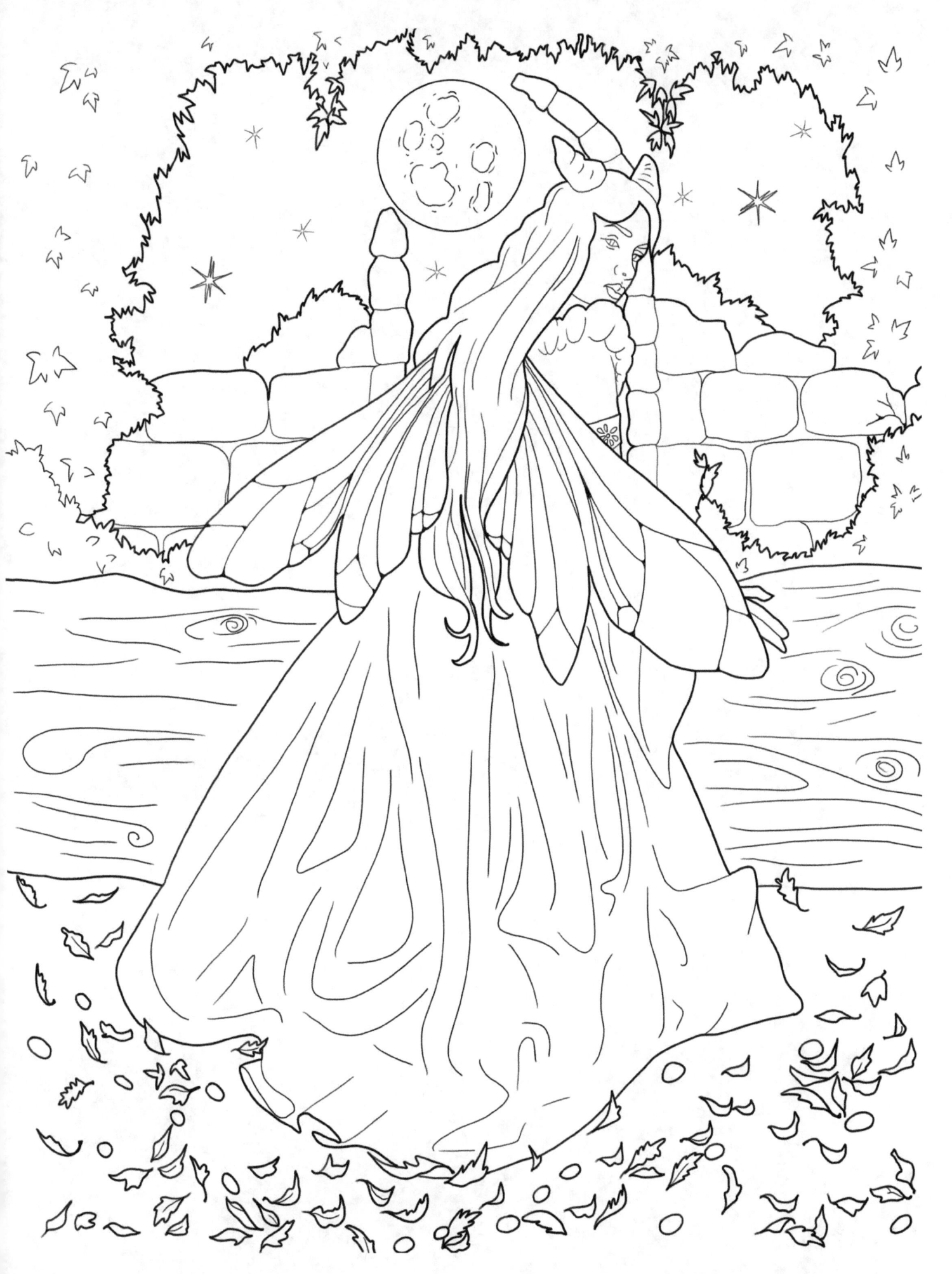

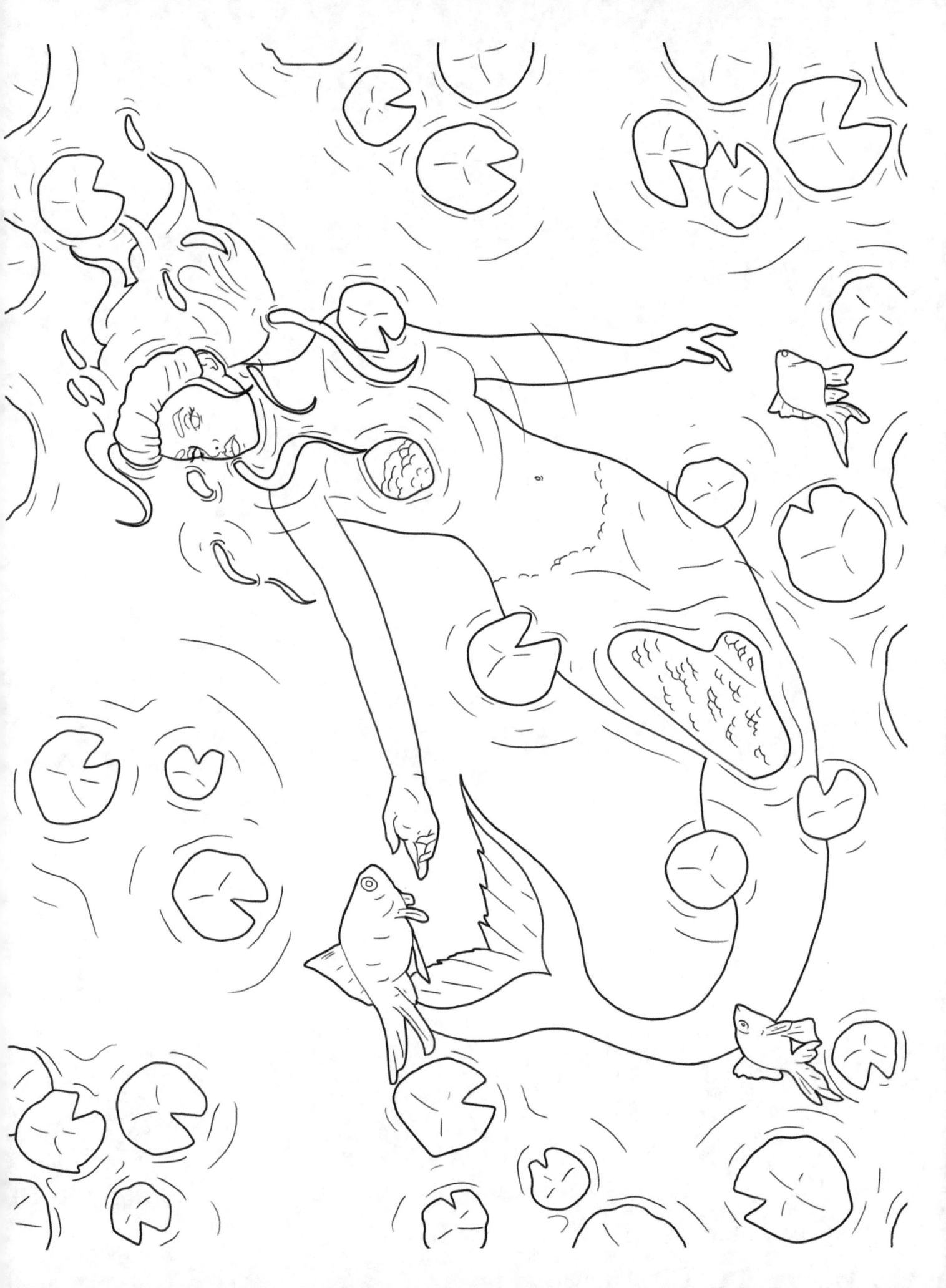

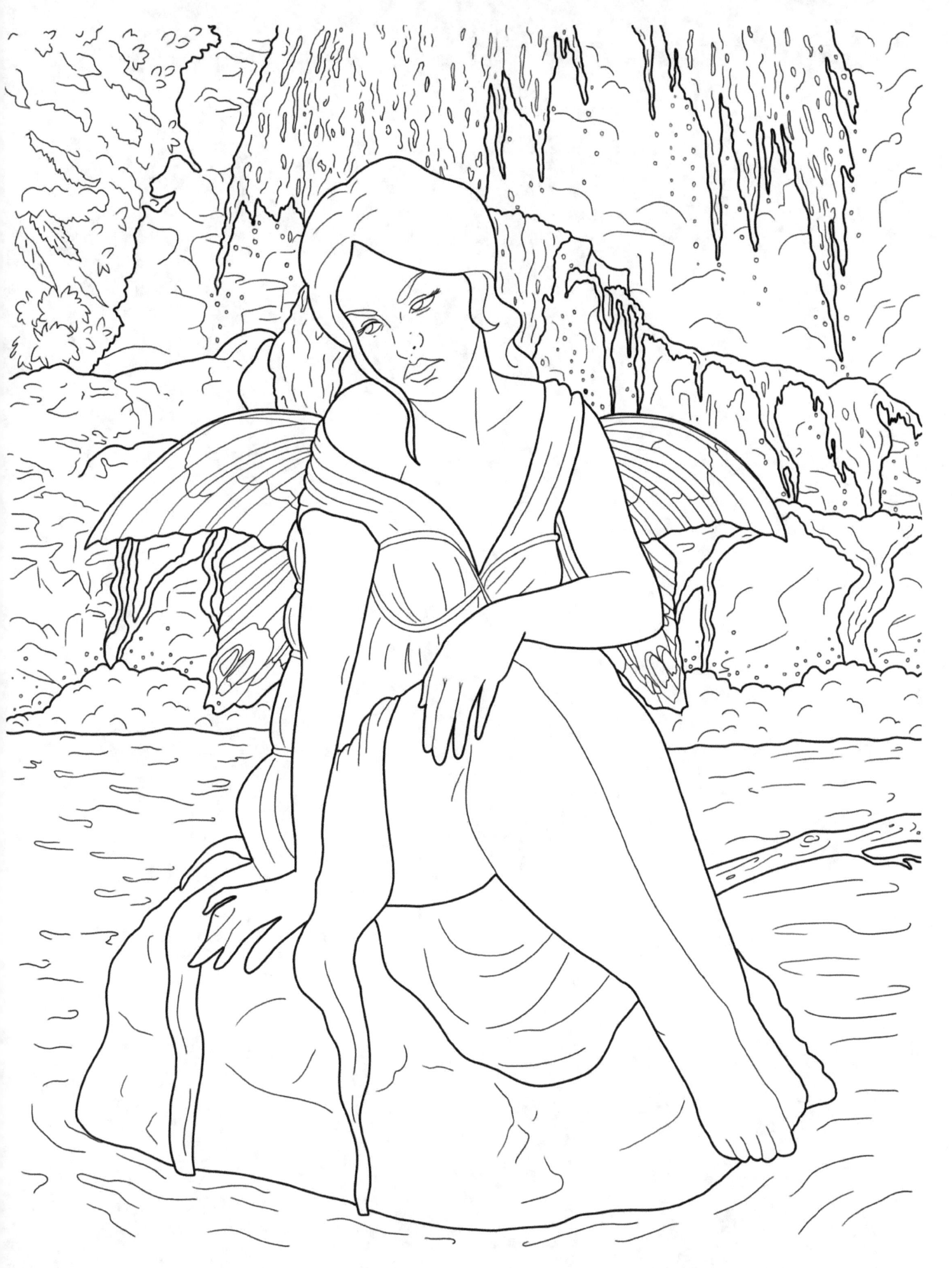

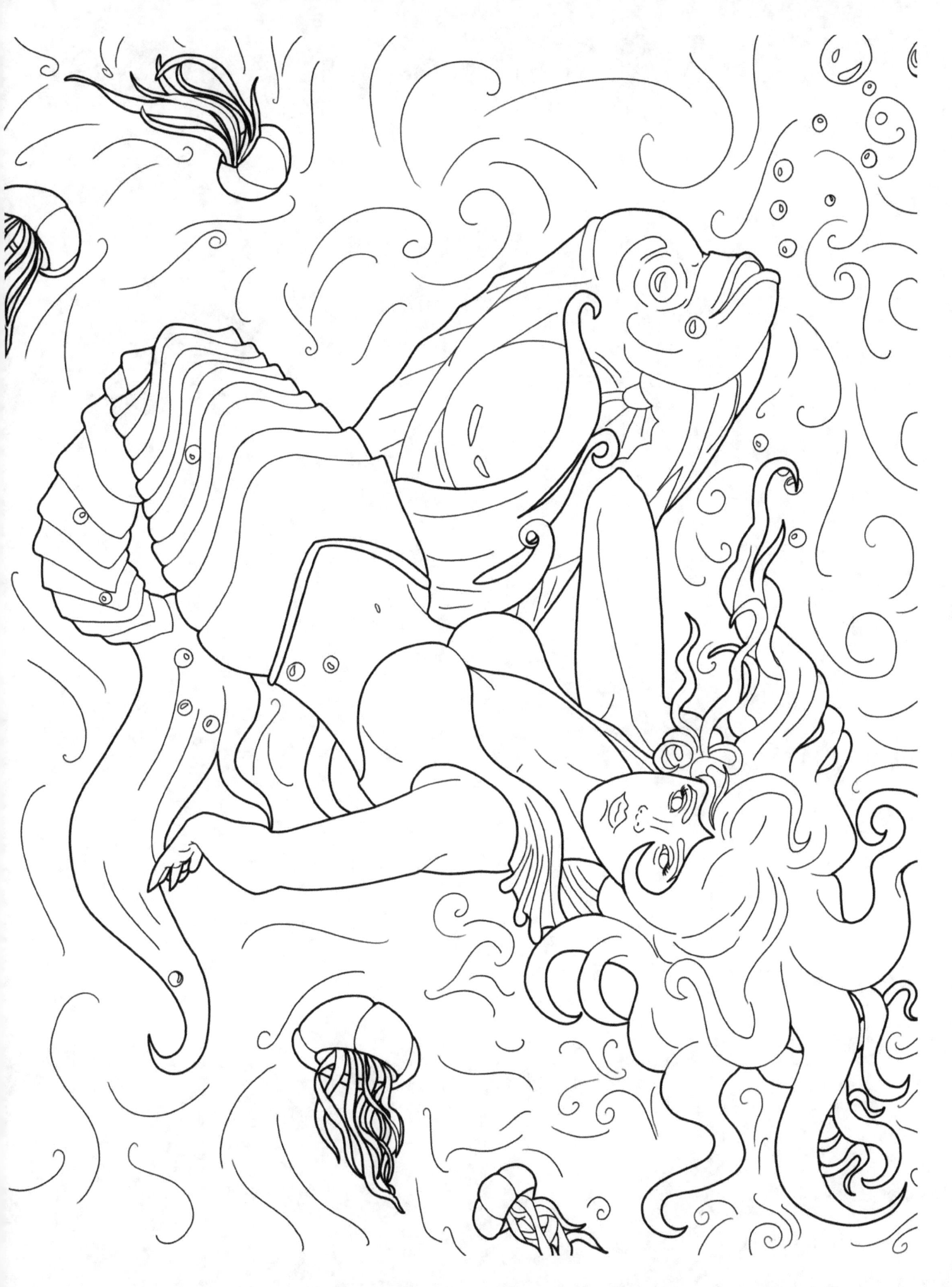

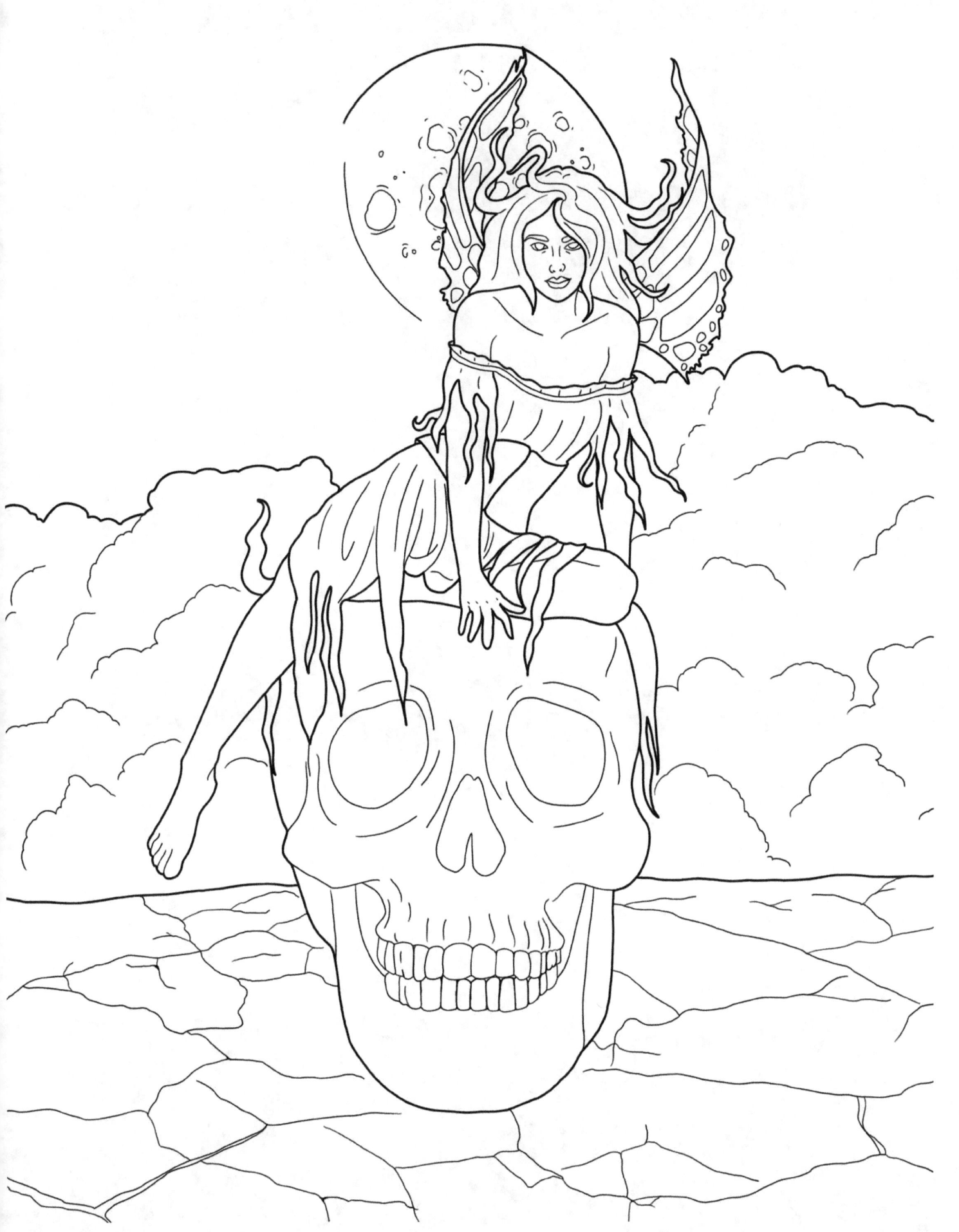

"MEMENTO MORI"

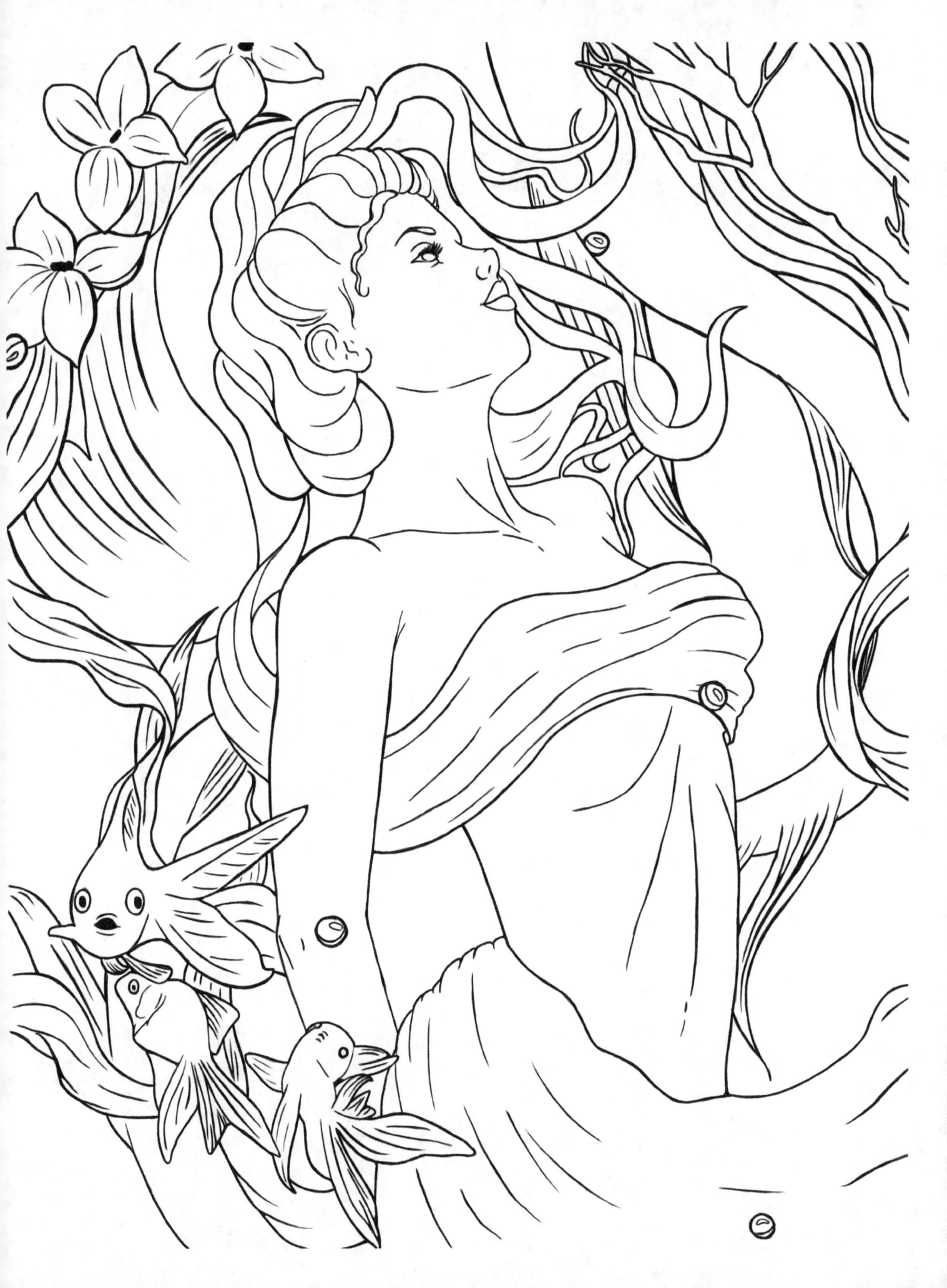

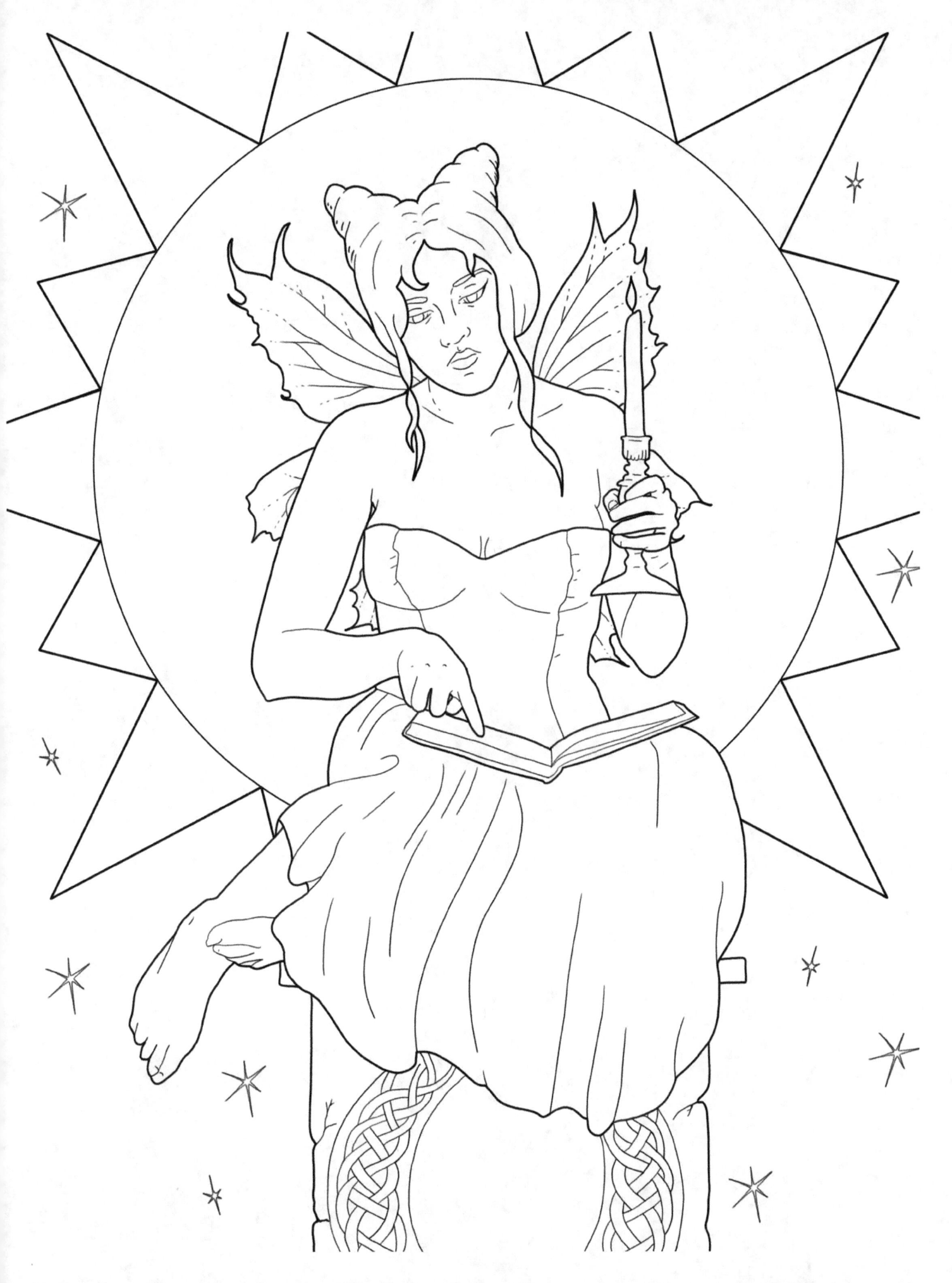

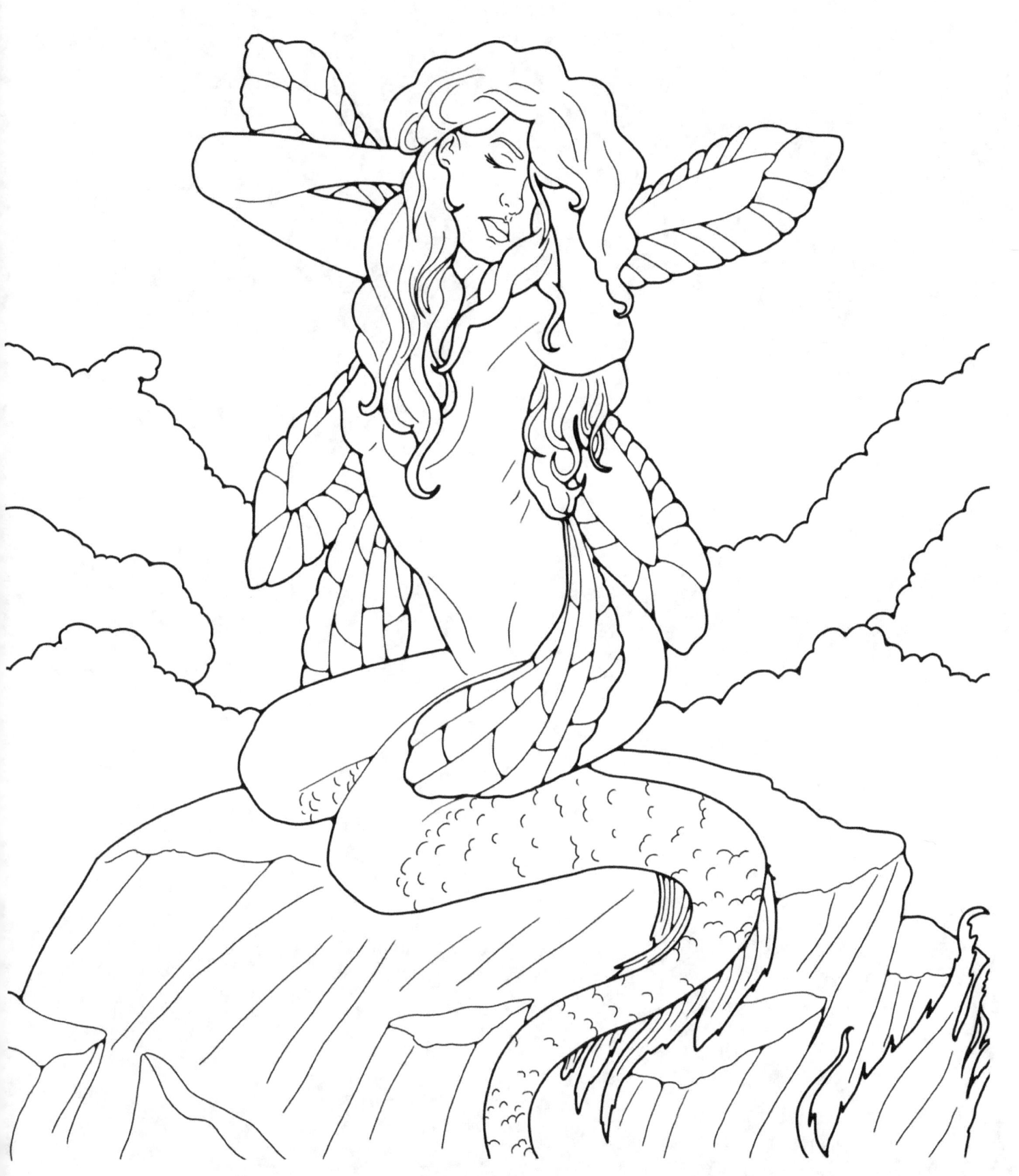

"OUT TO DRY"

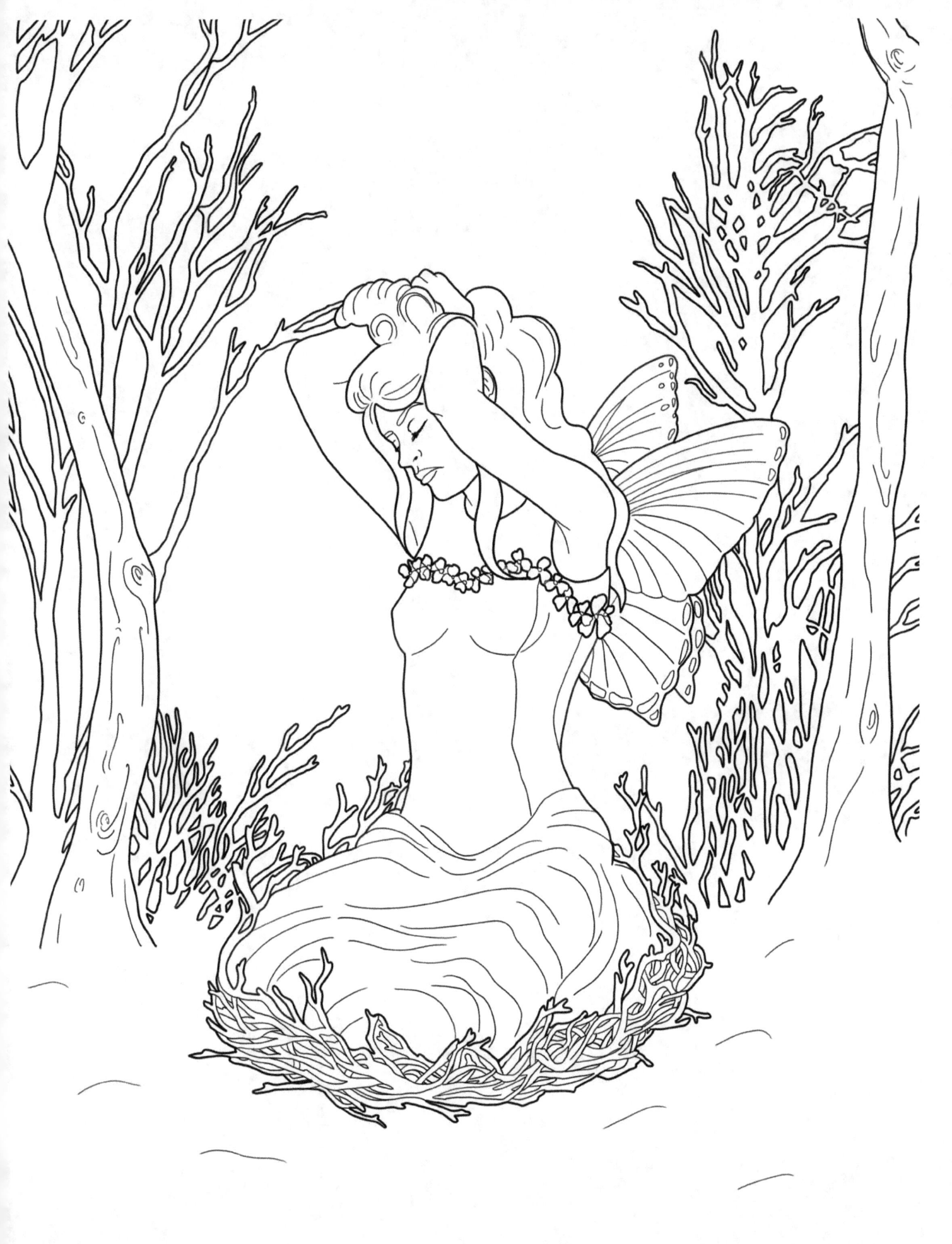

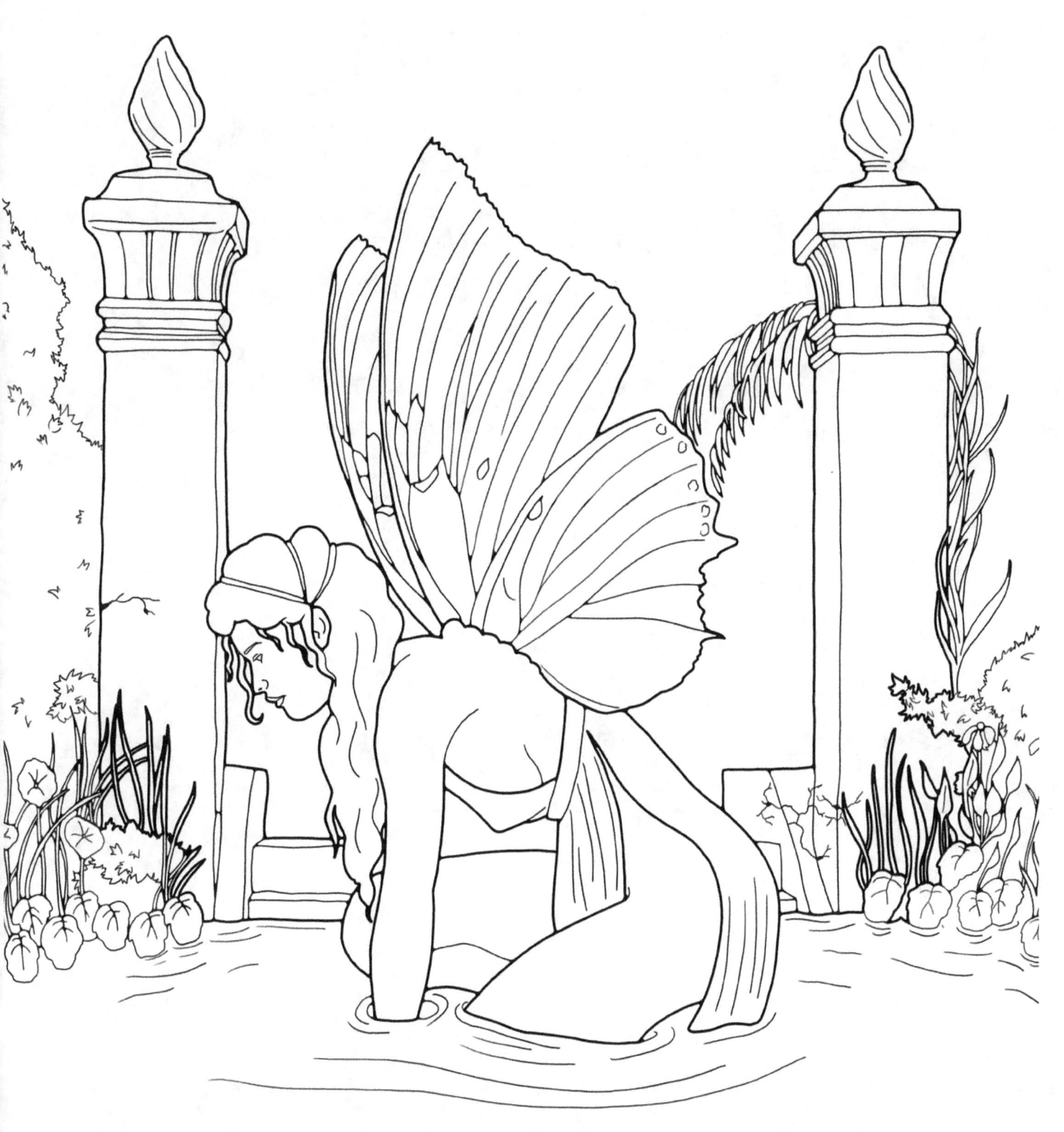

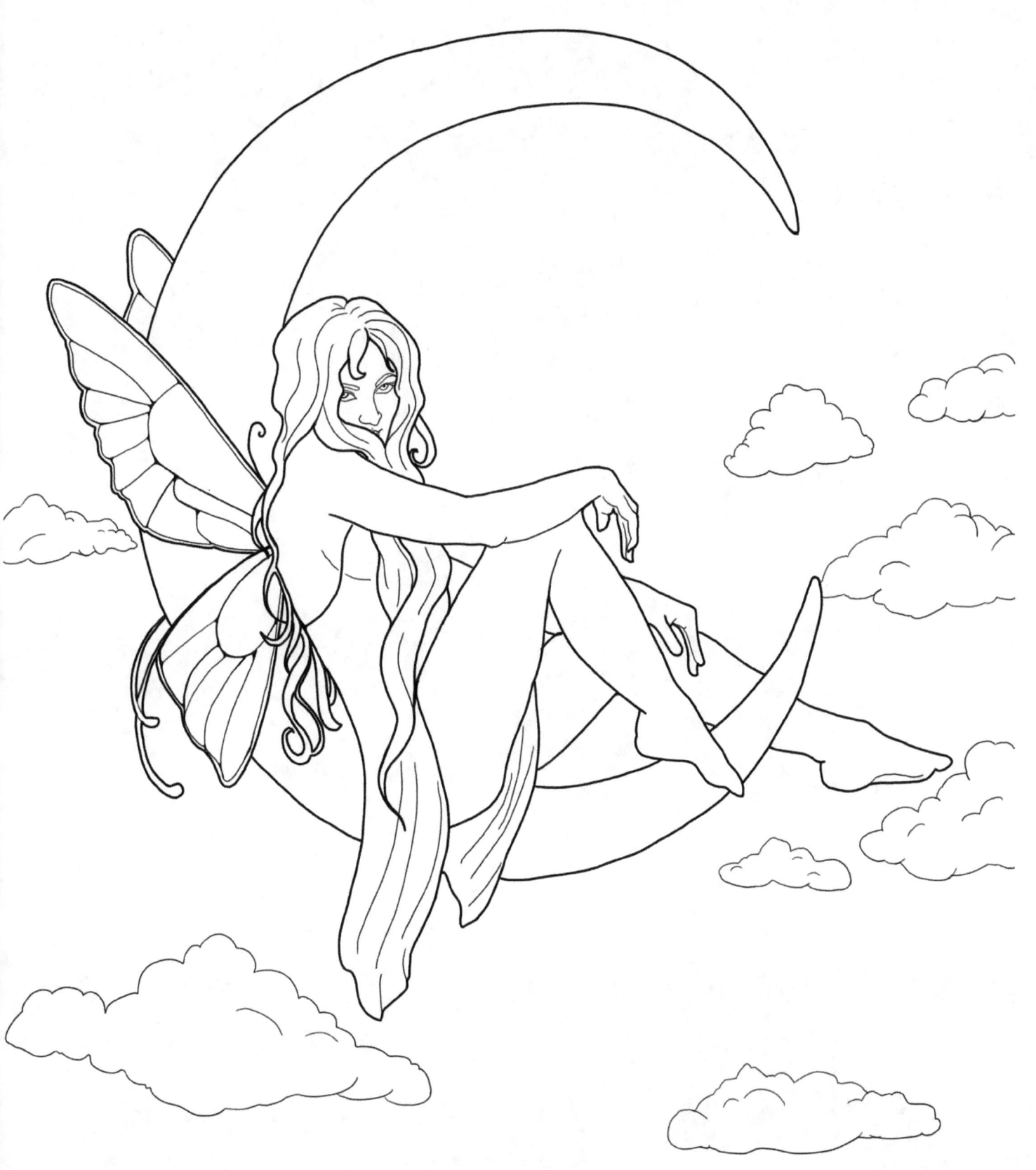

"WINTER MOON"

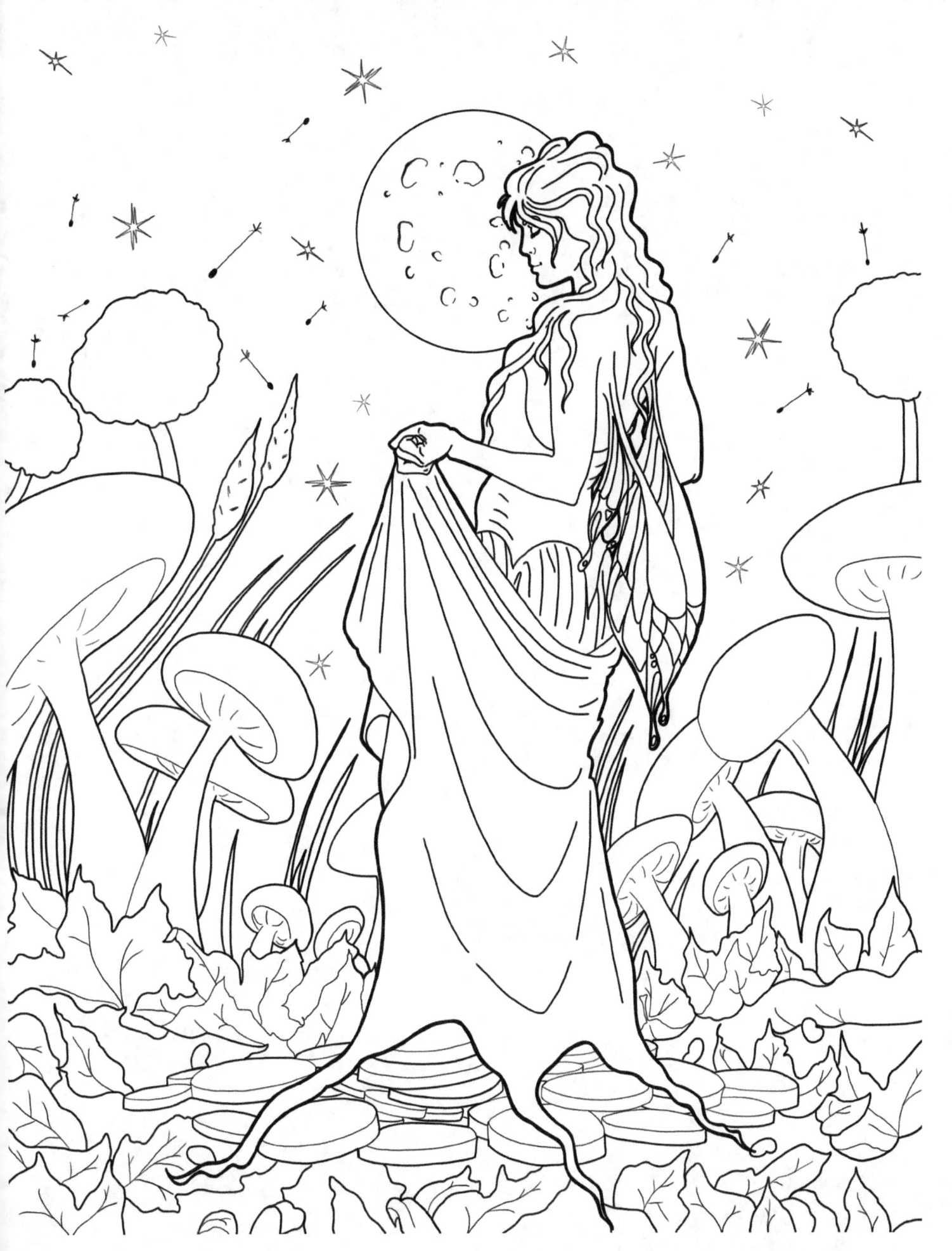

"TRICKY TREASURES"

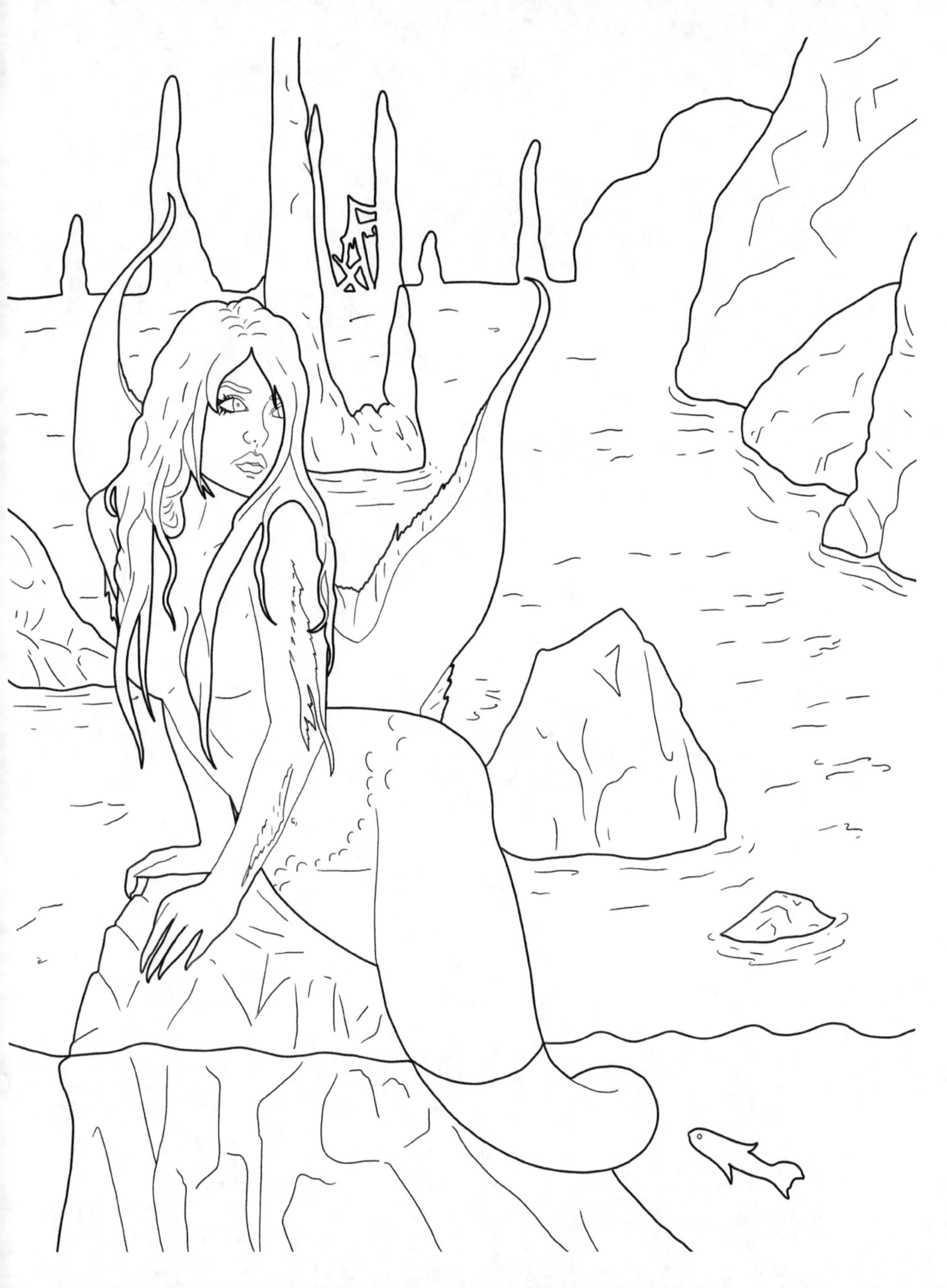

"SIREN'S SONG"

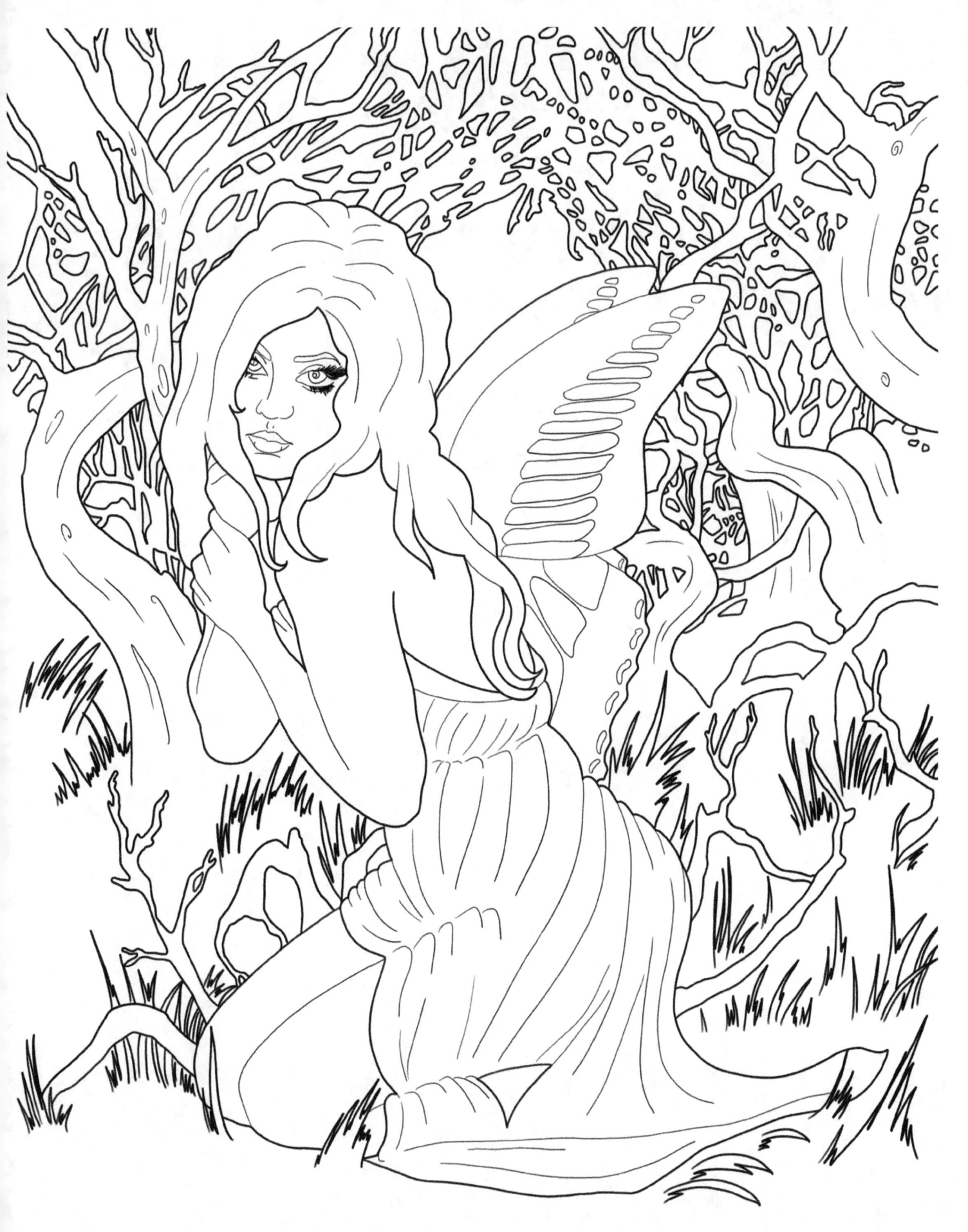

"BLUEBOTTLE"

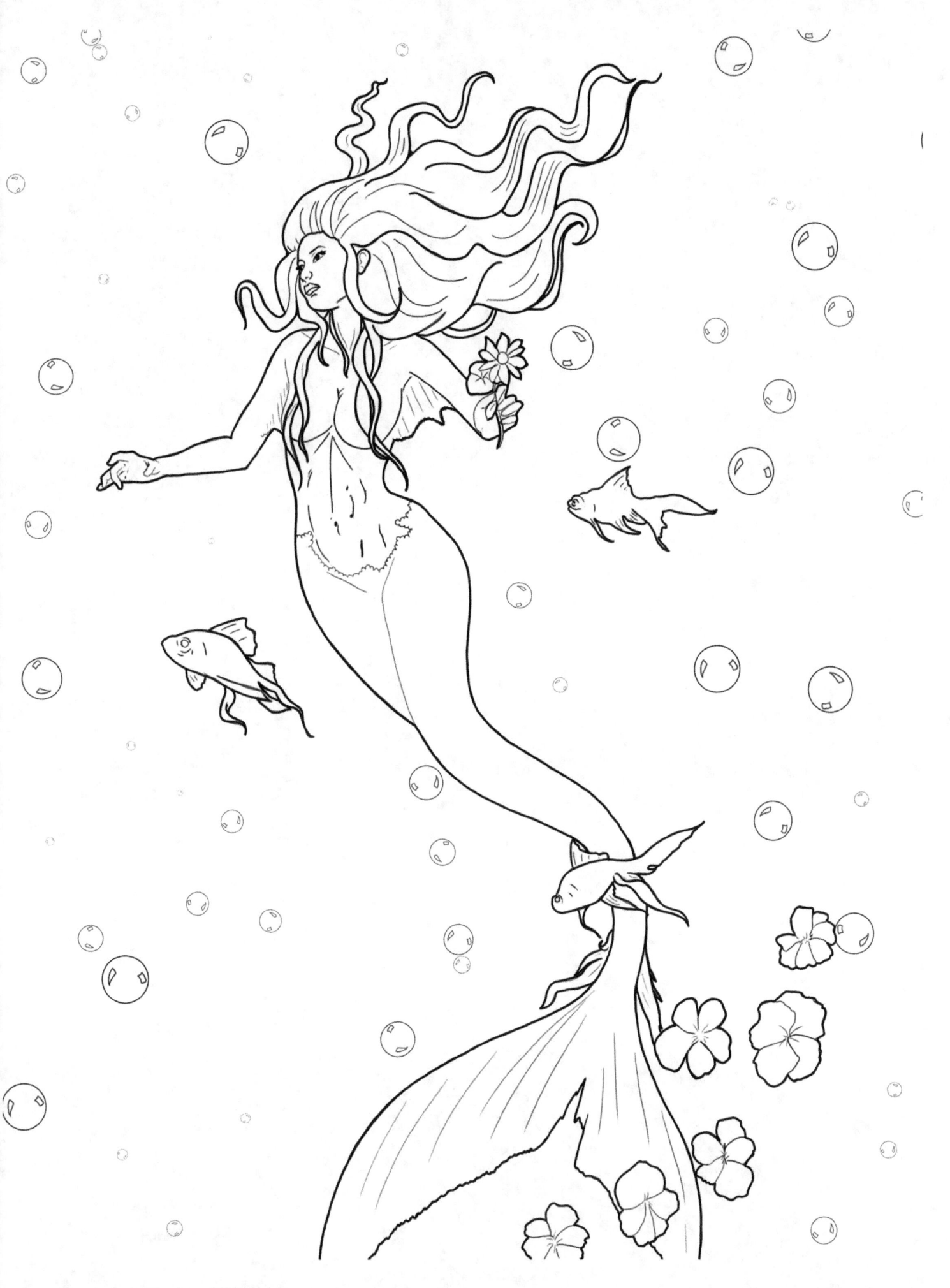

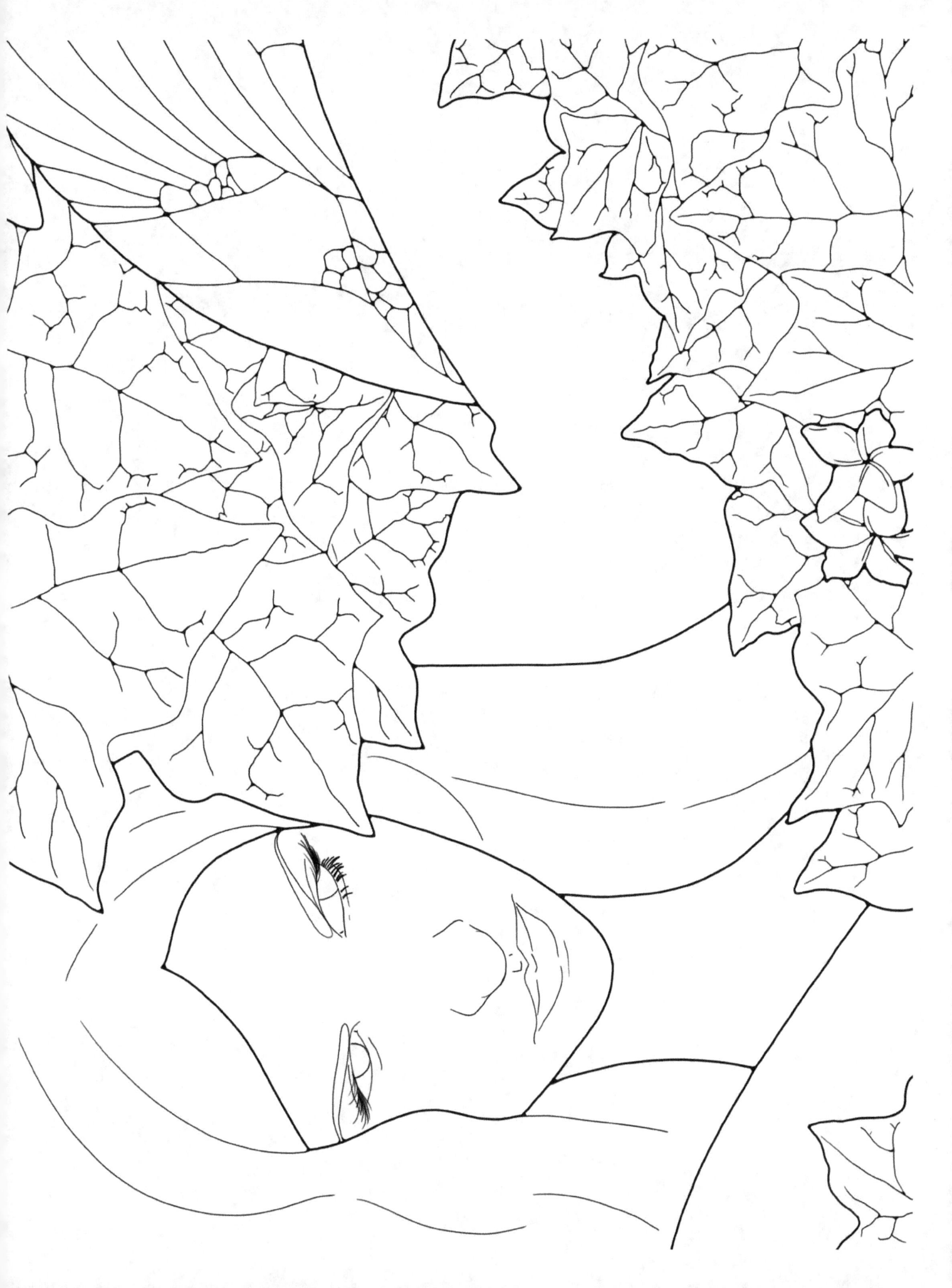

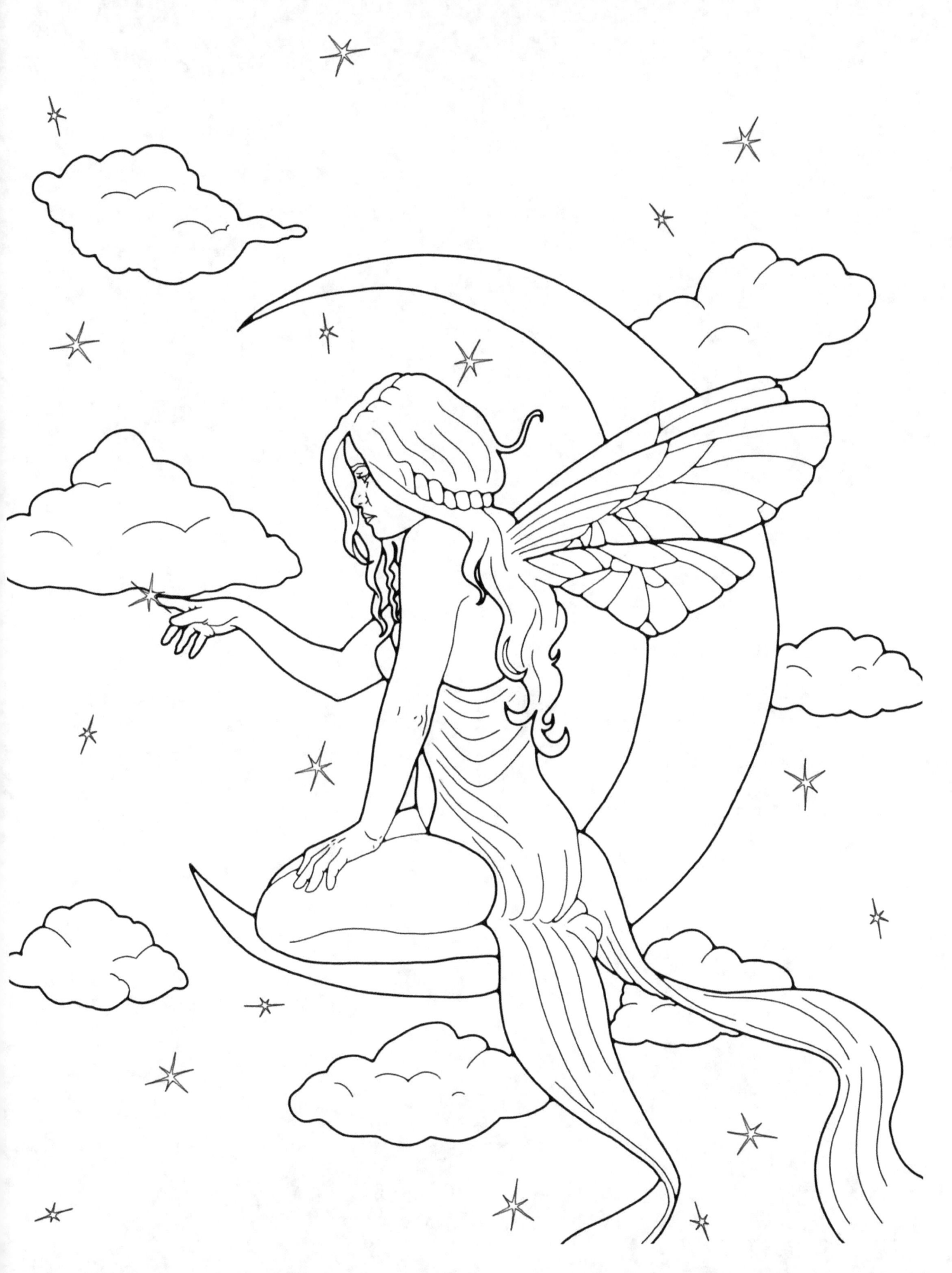

"FIREFLY MOON"

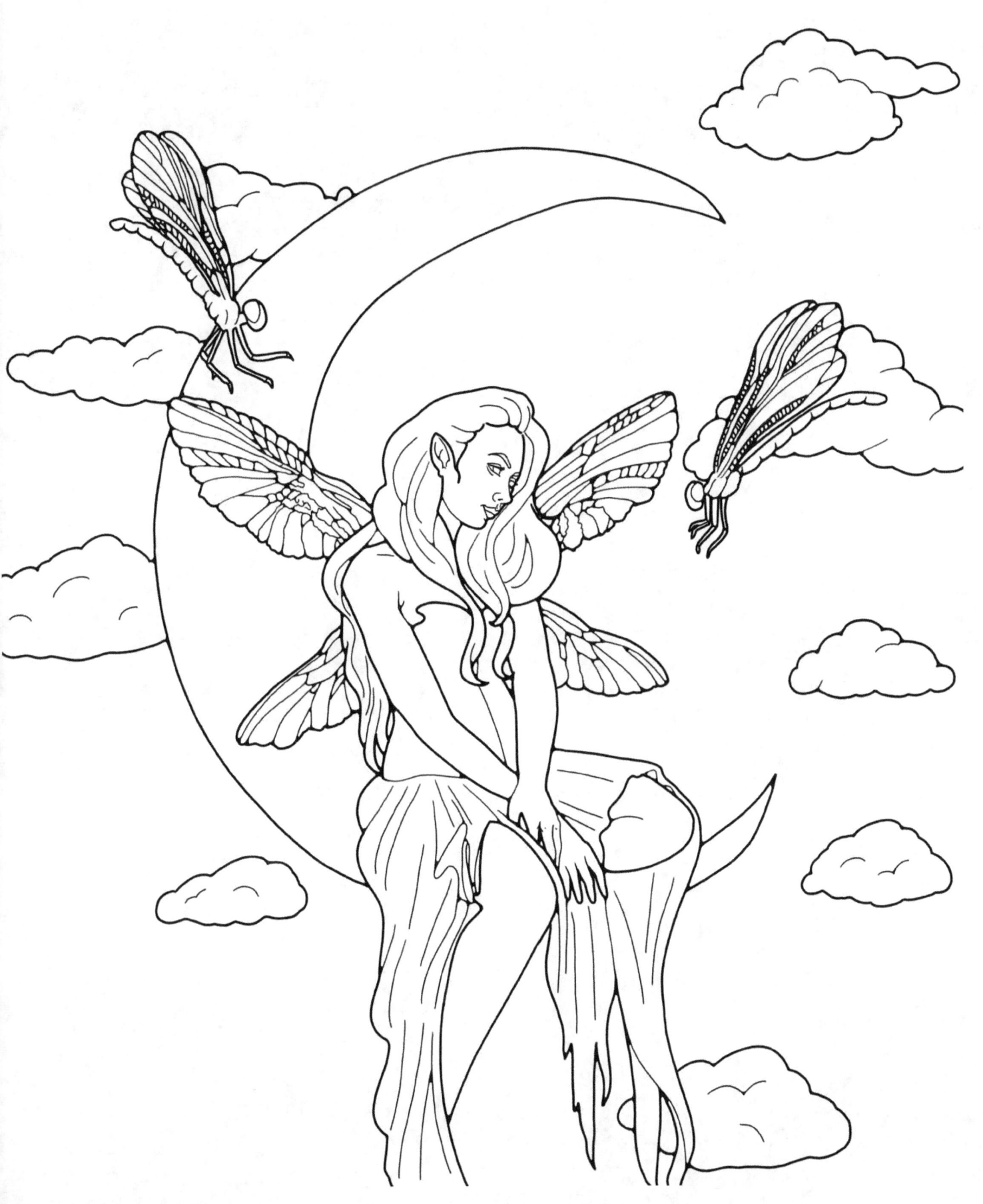

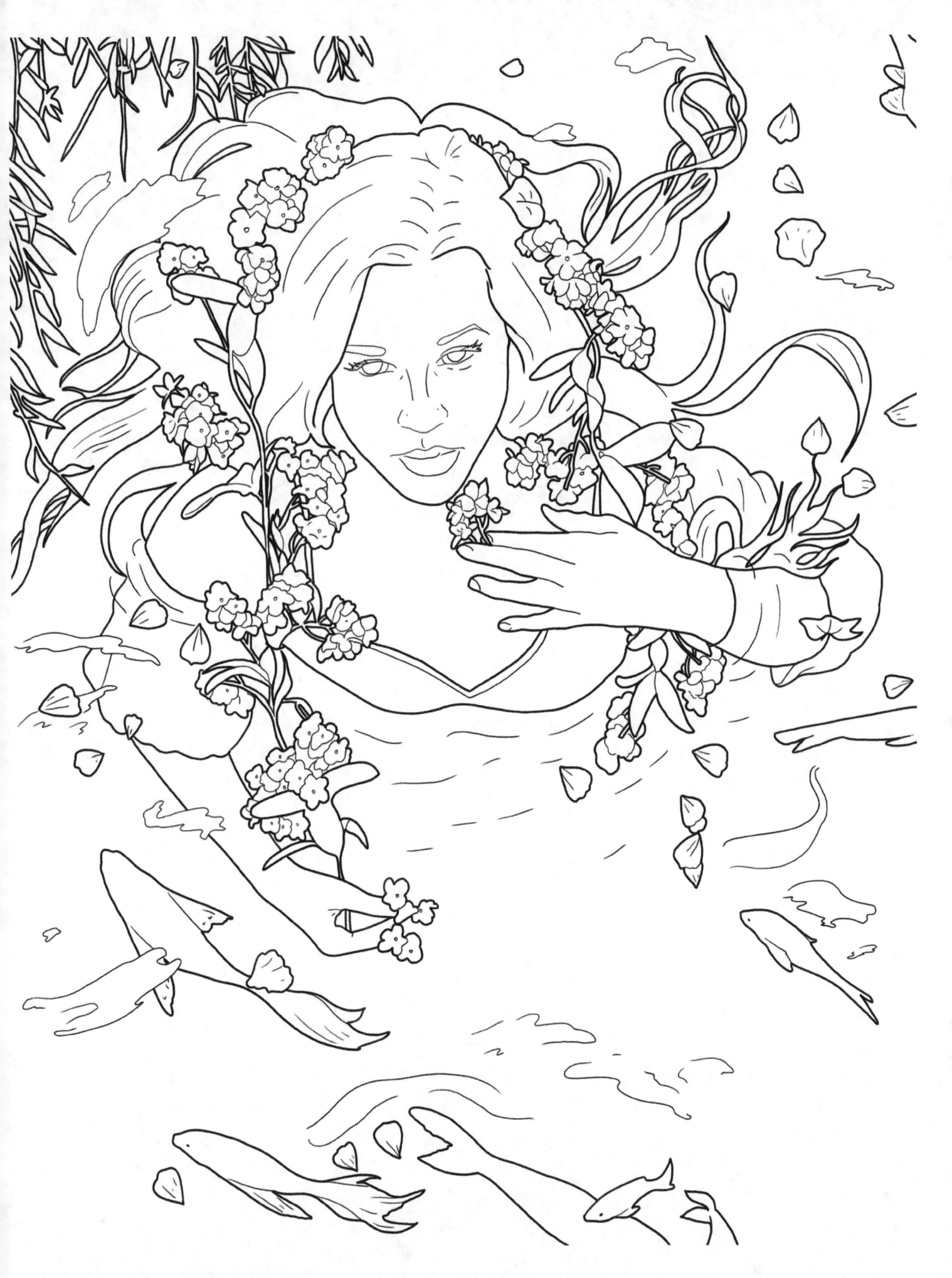

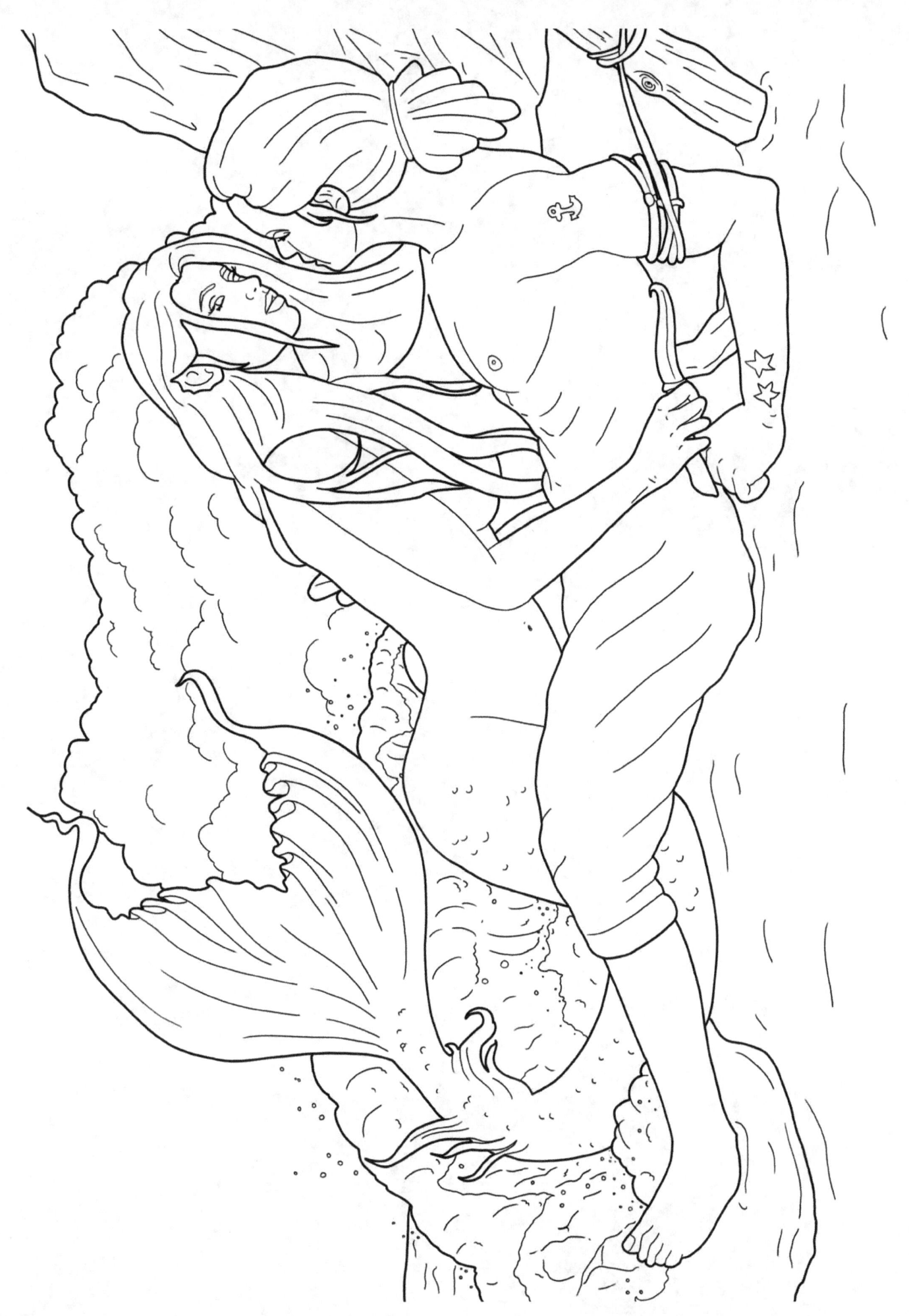

"THE SIREN'S CATCH"

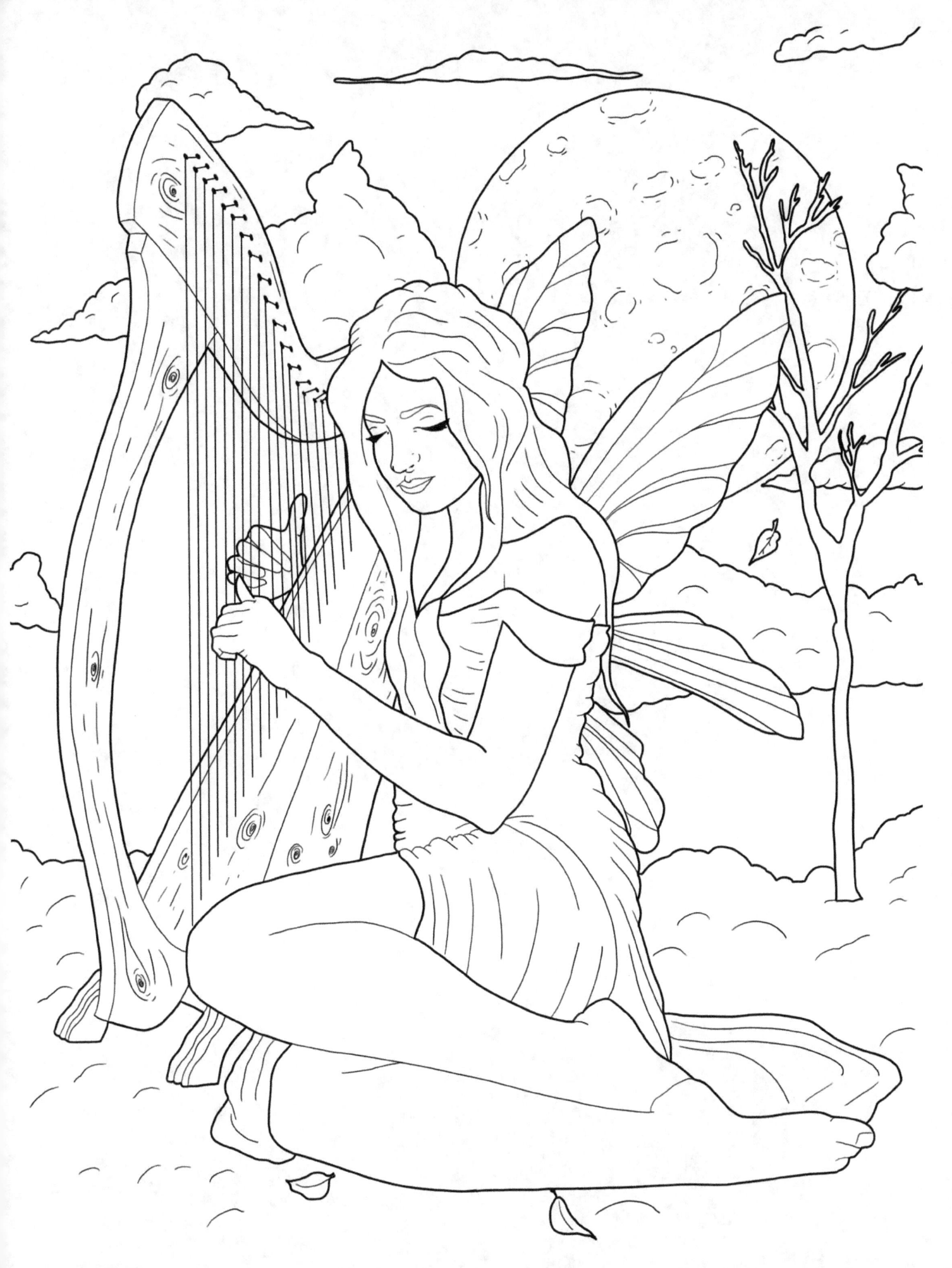

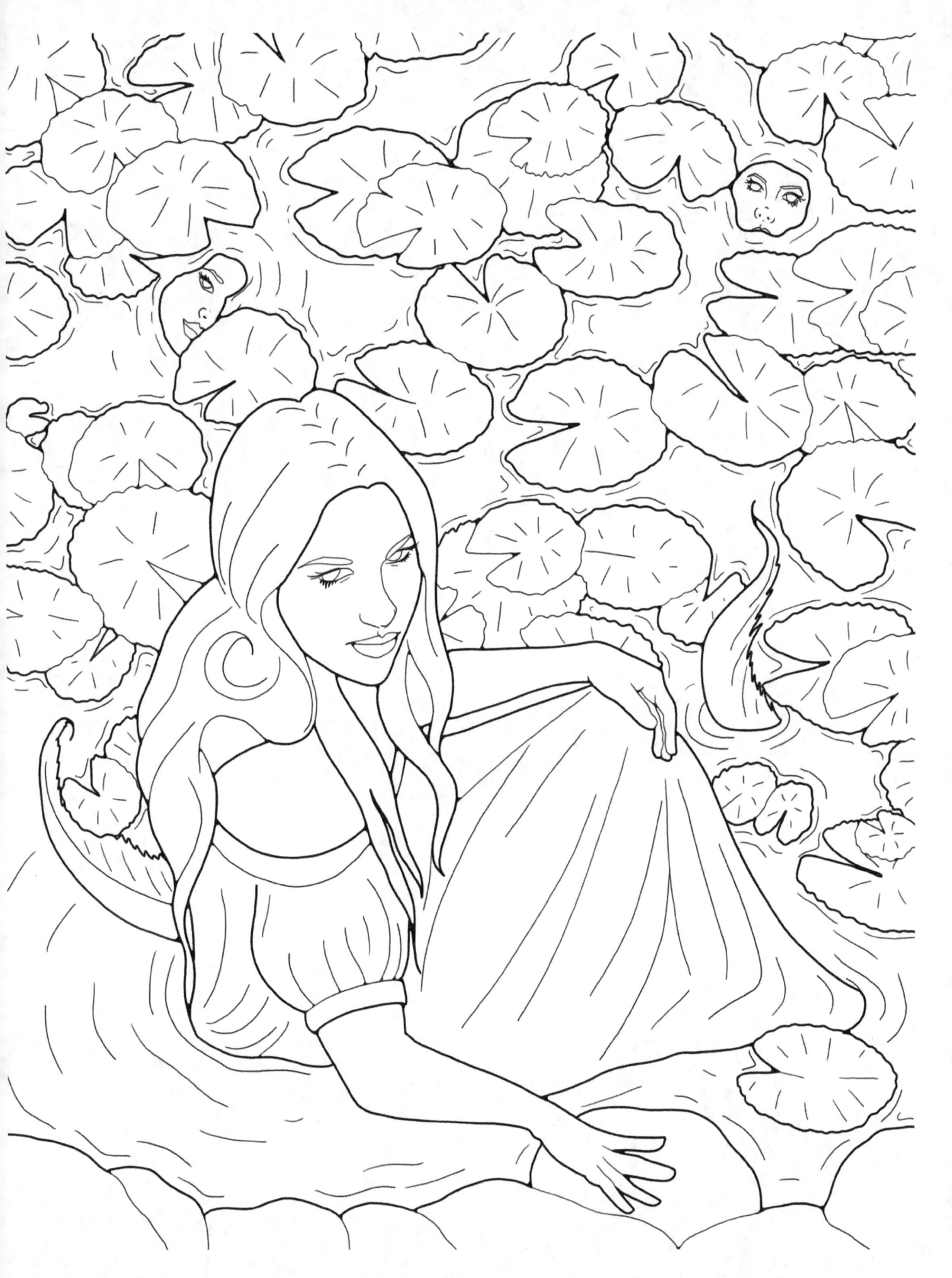

"JOIN US."

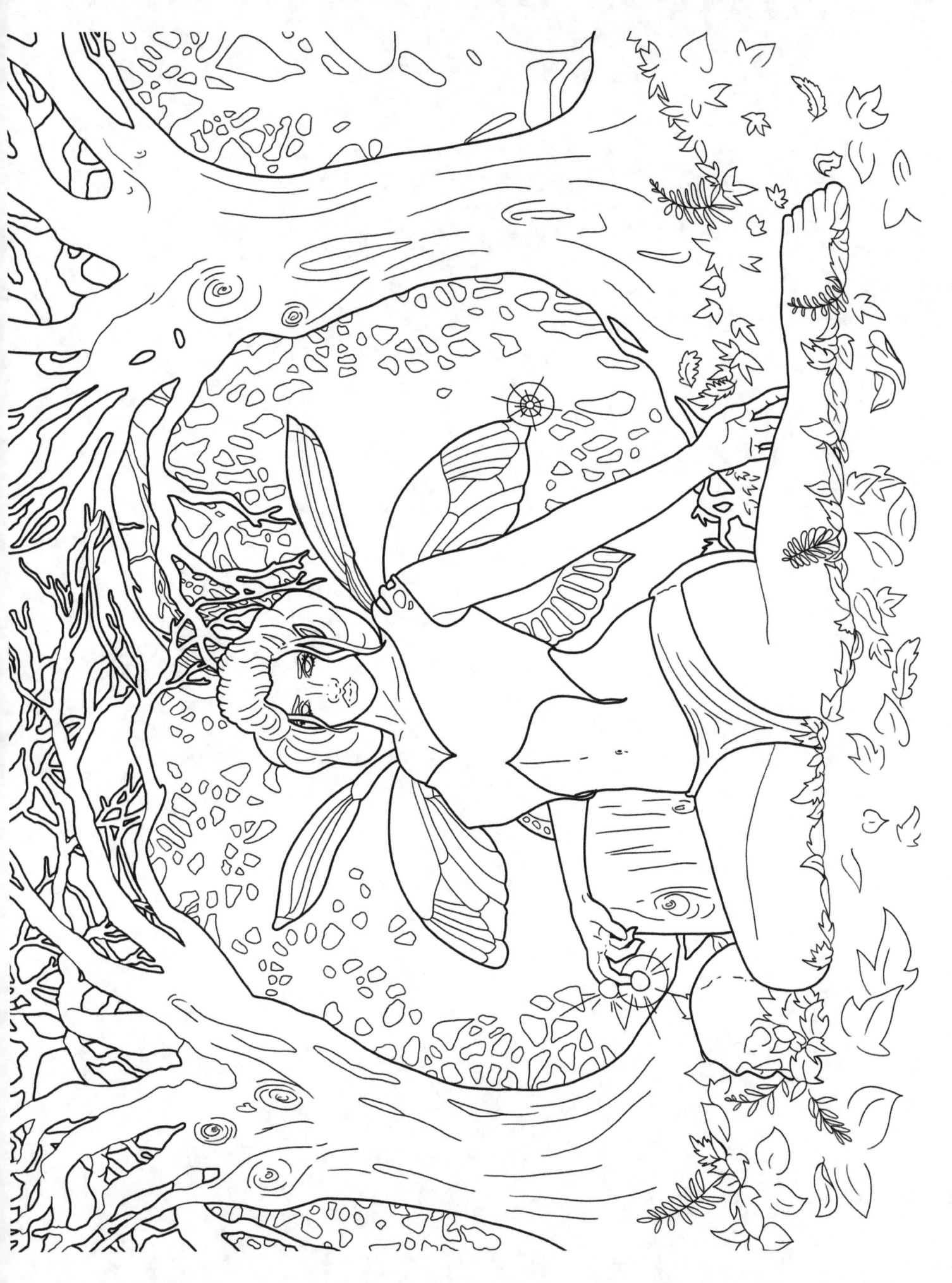

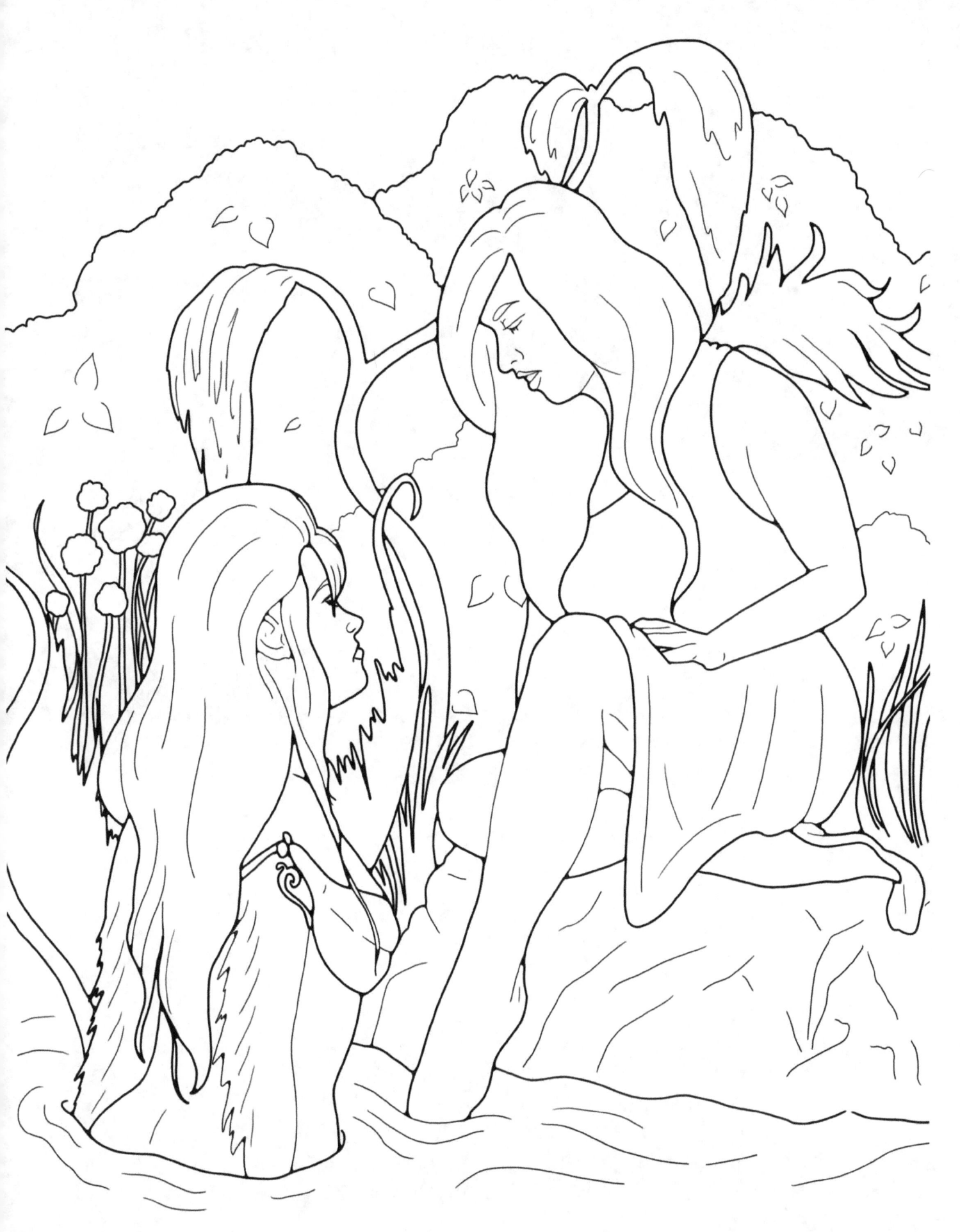

"WORLDS APART"

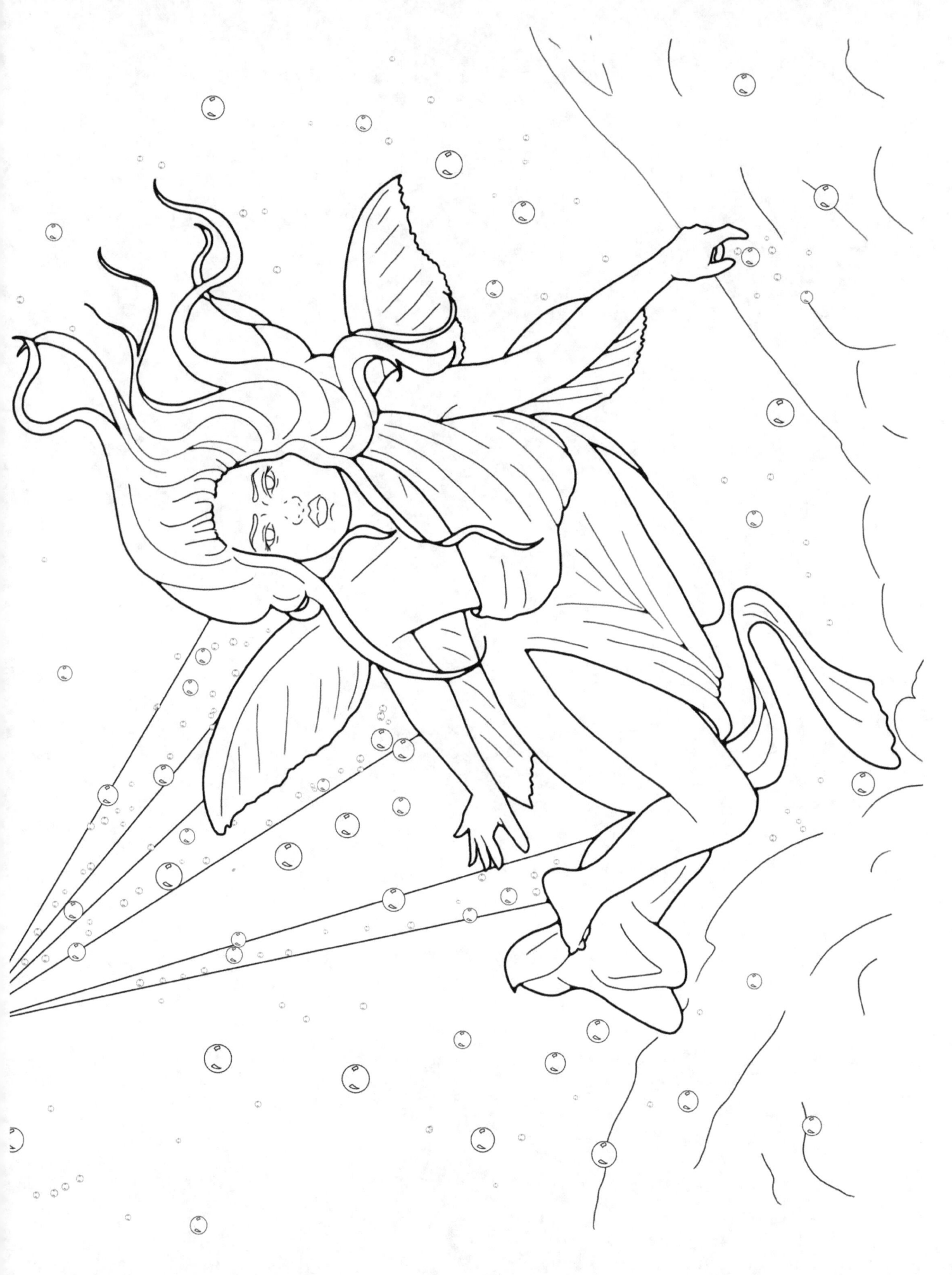

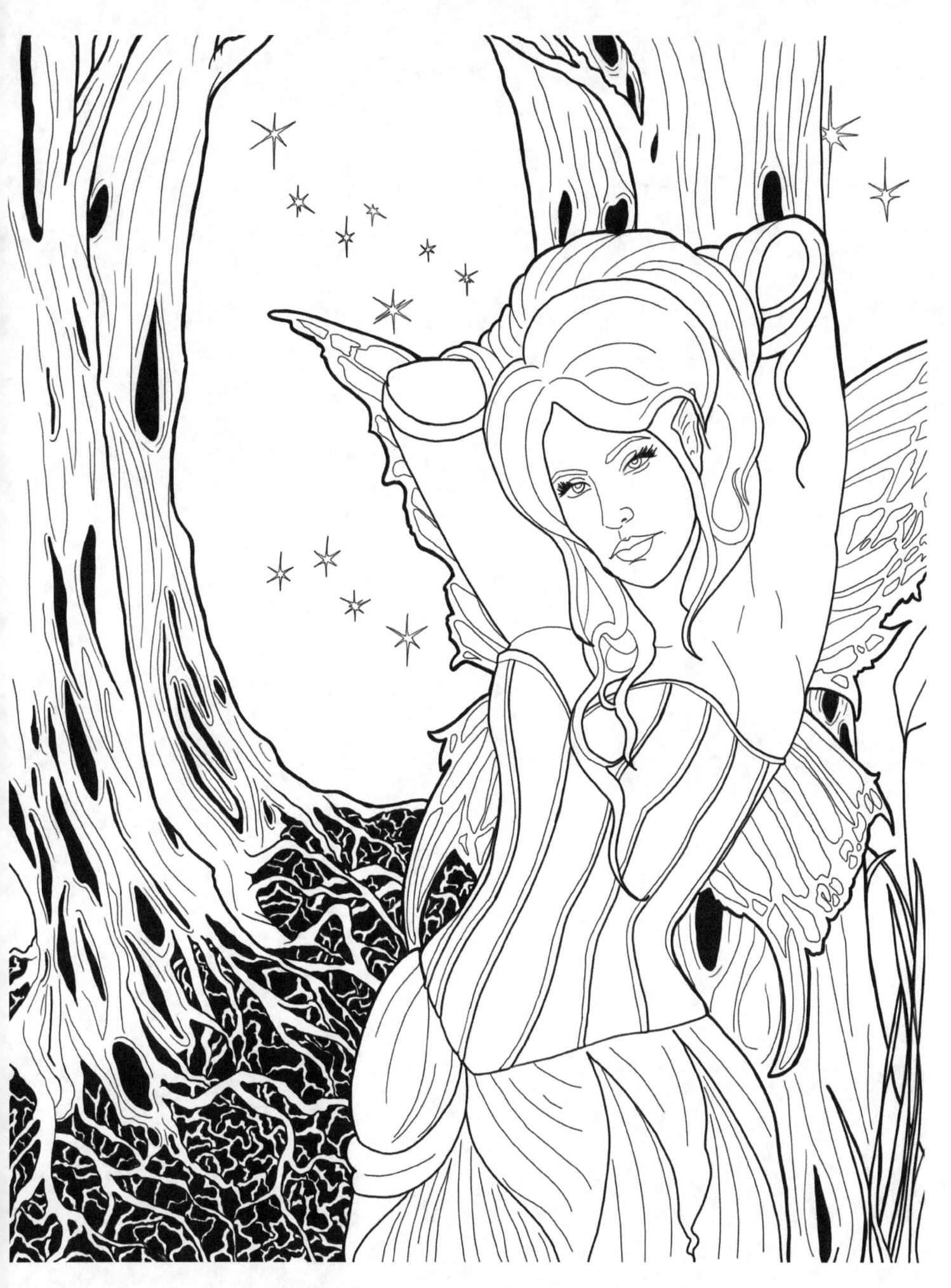

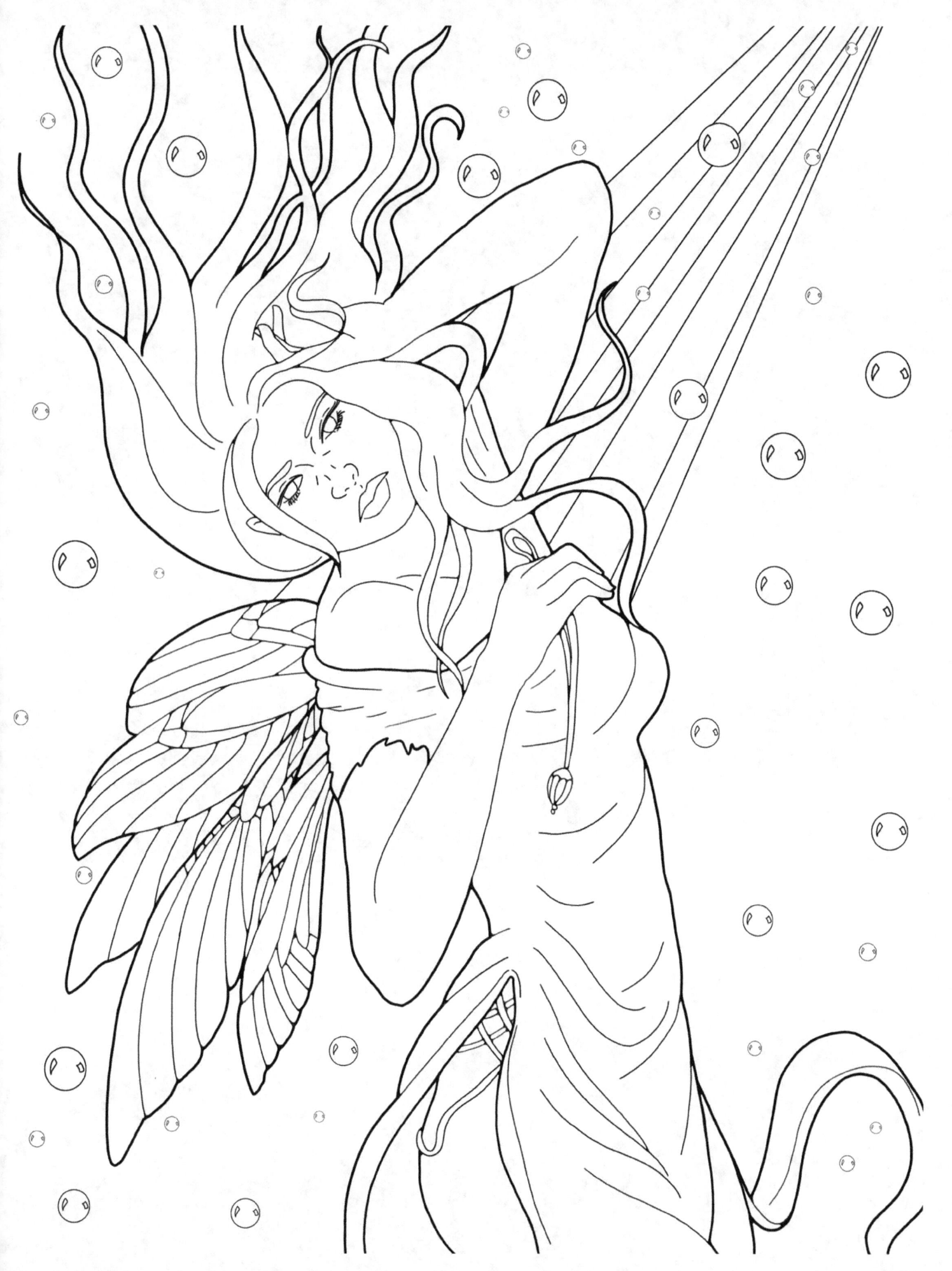

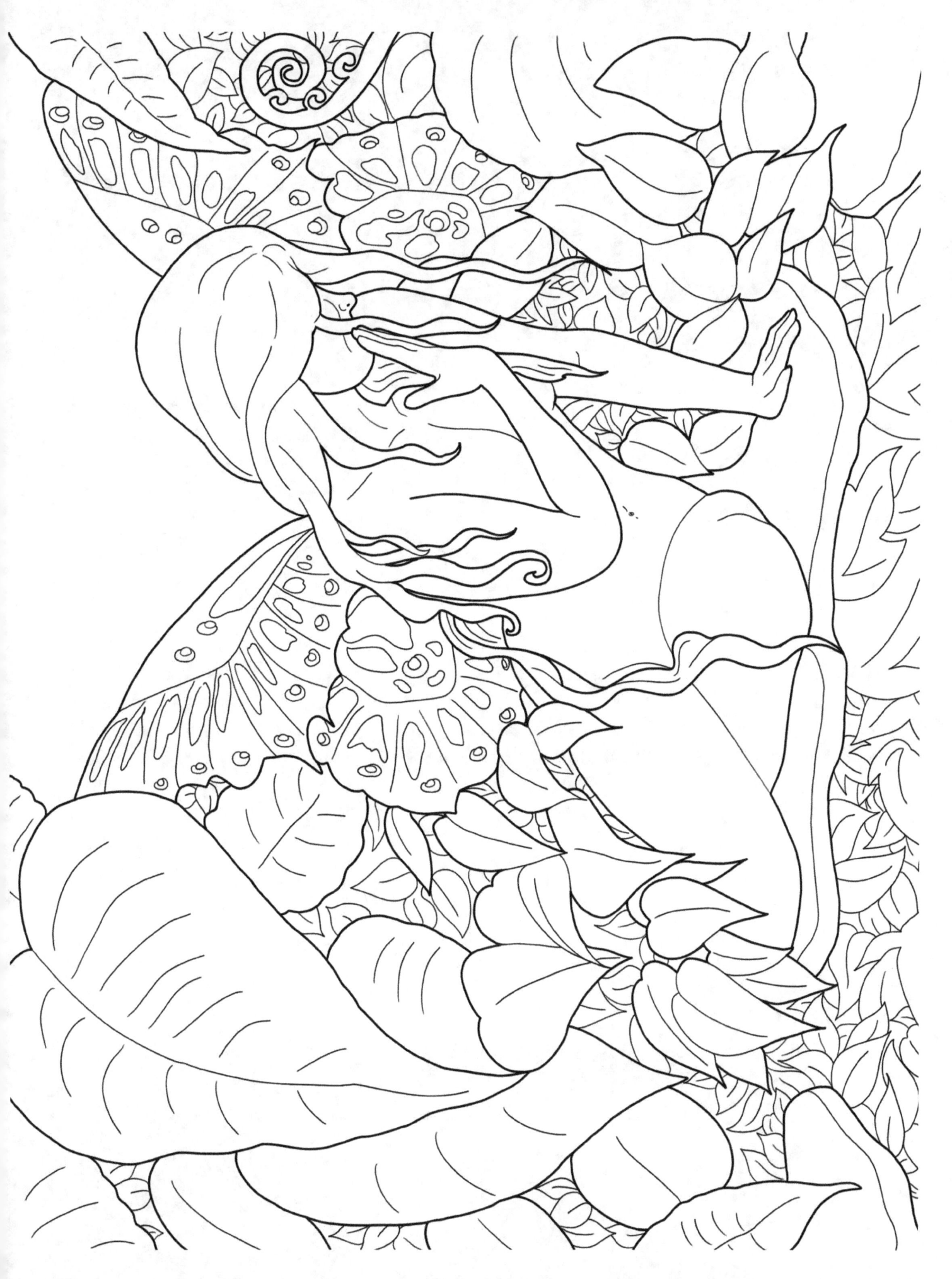

"SHY"

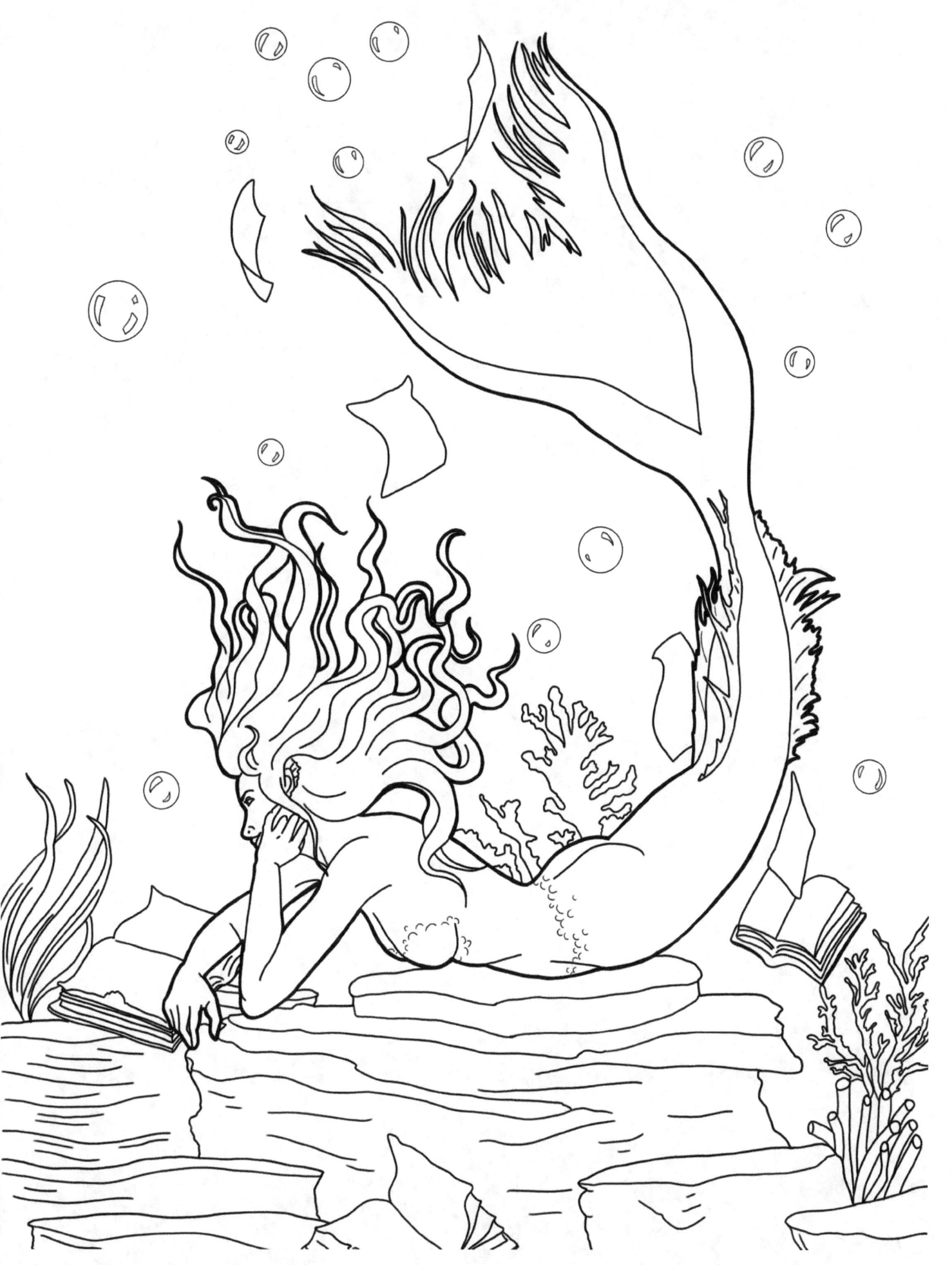

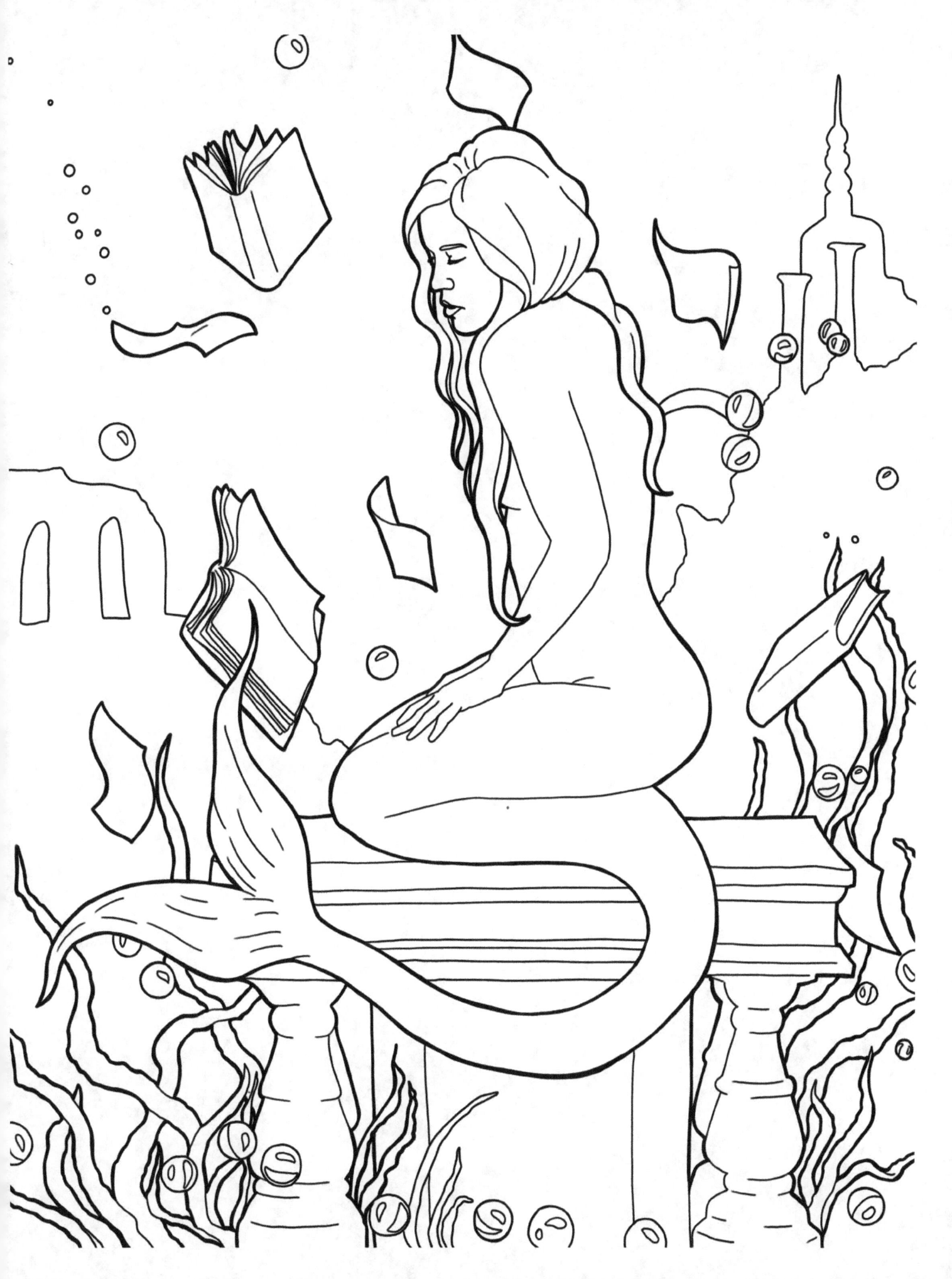

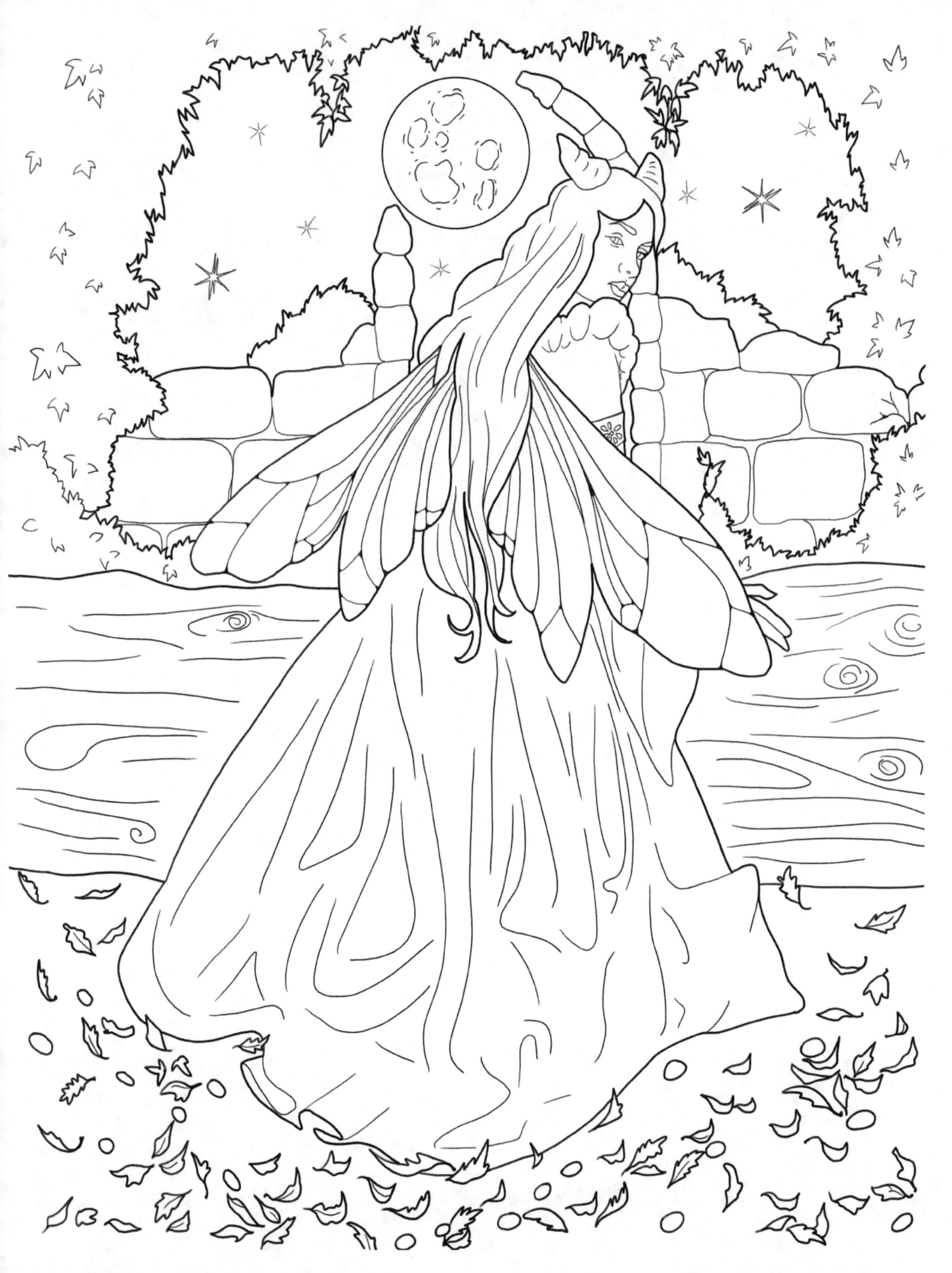

"FOLLOW ME"

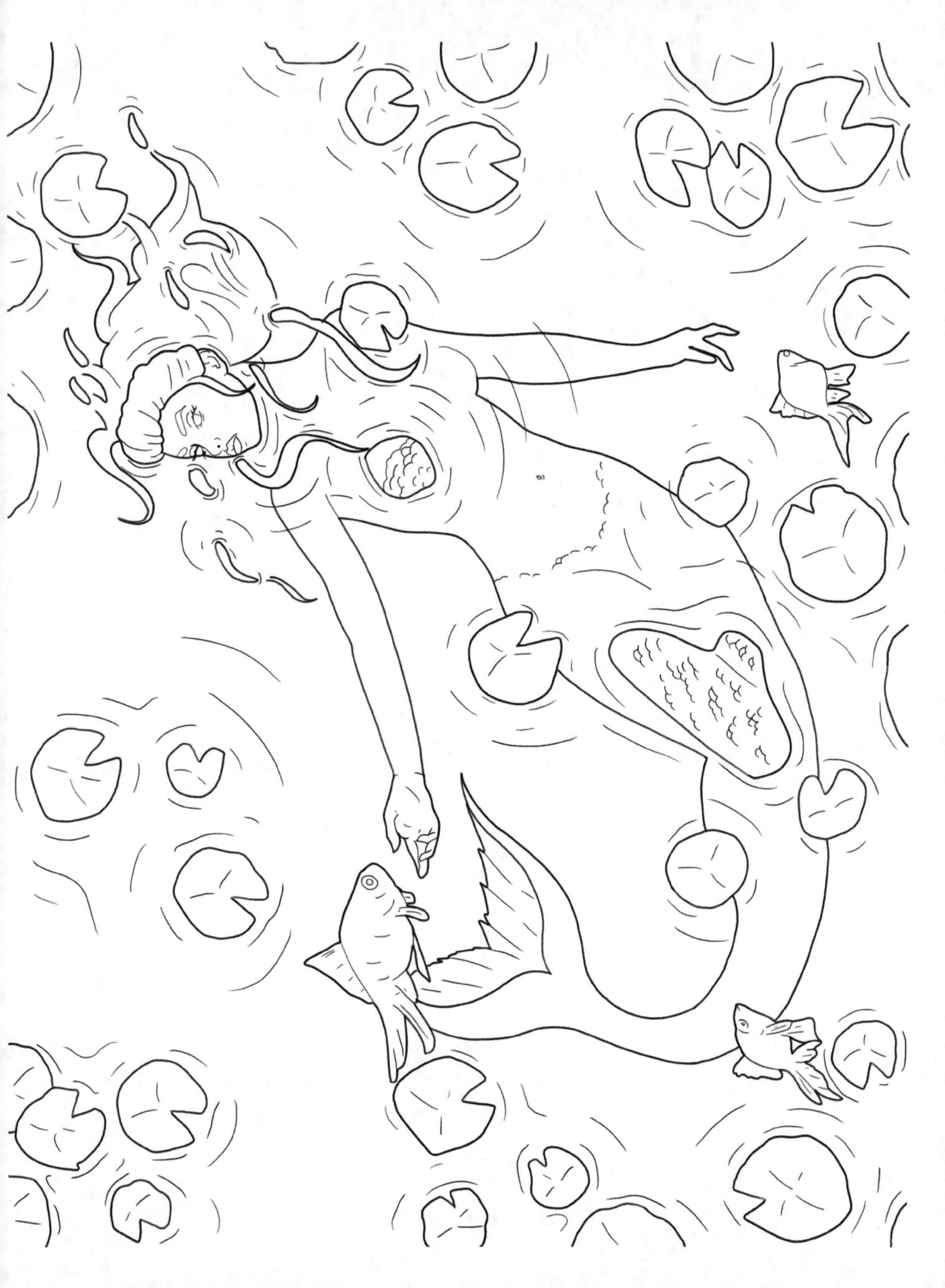

"GOLDFISH MERMAID"

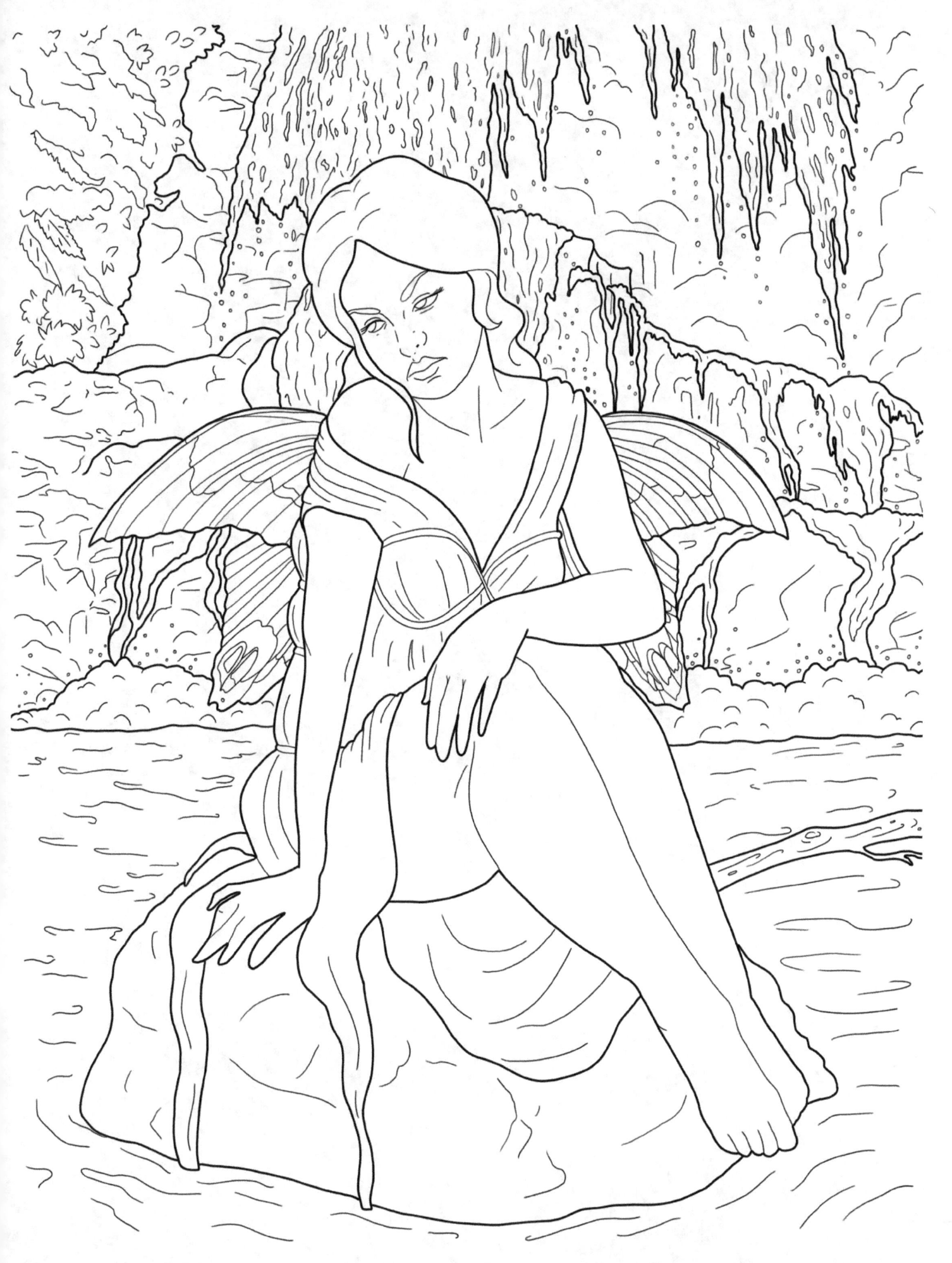

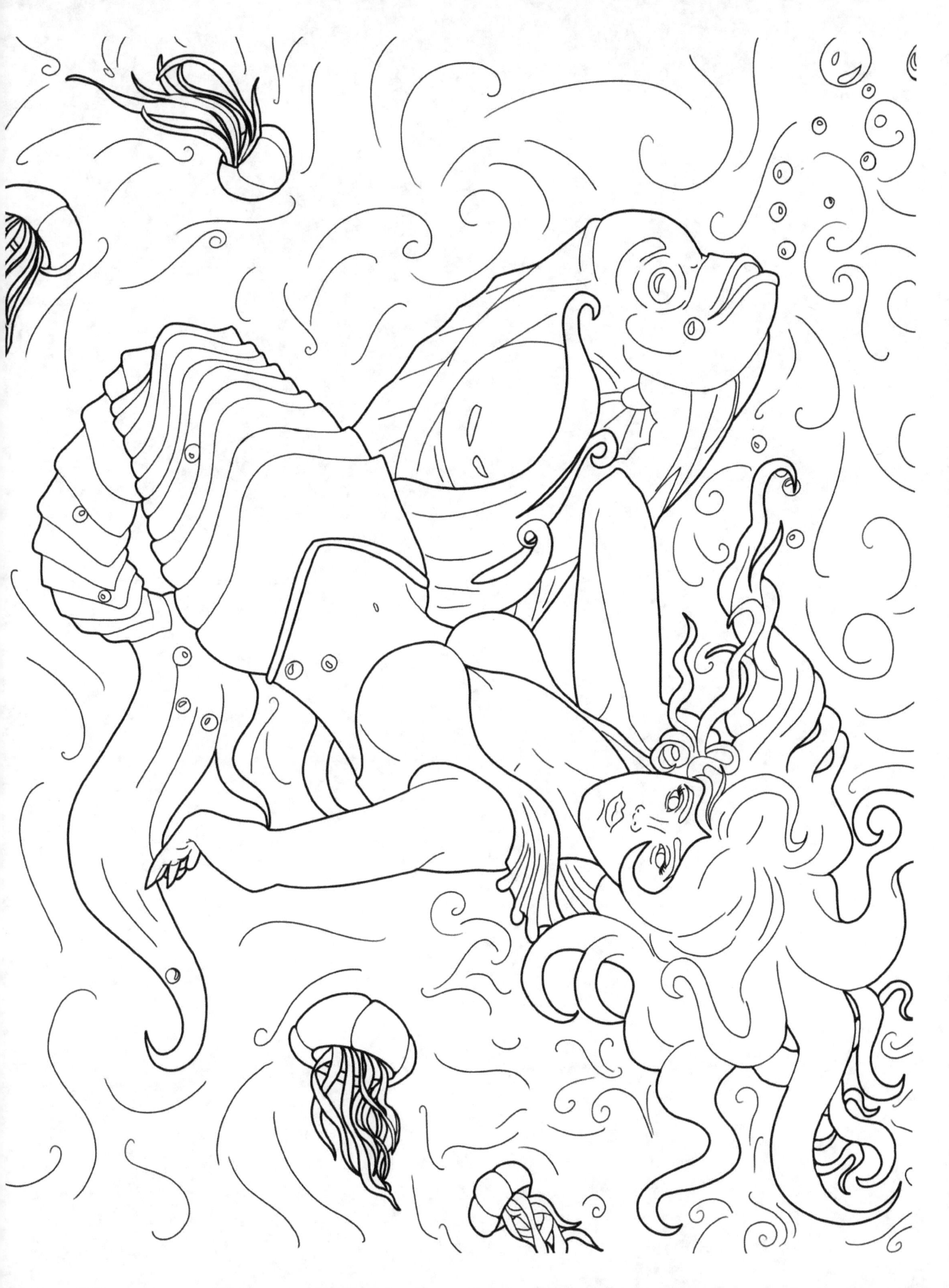

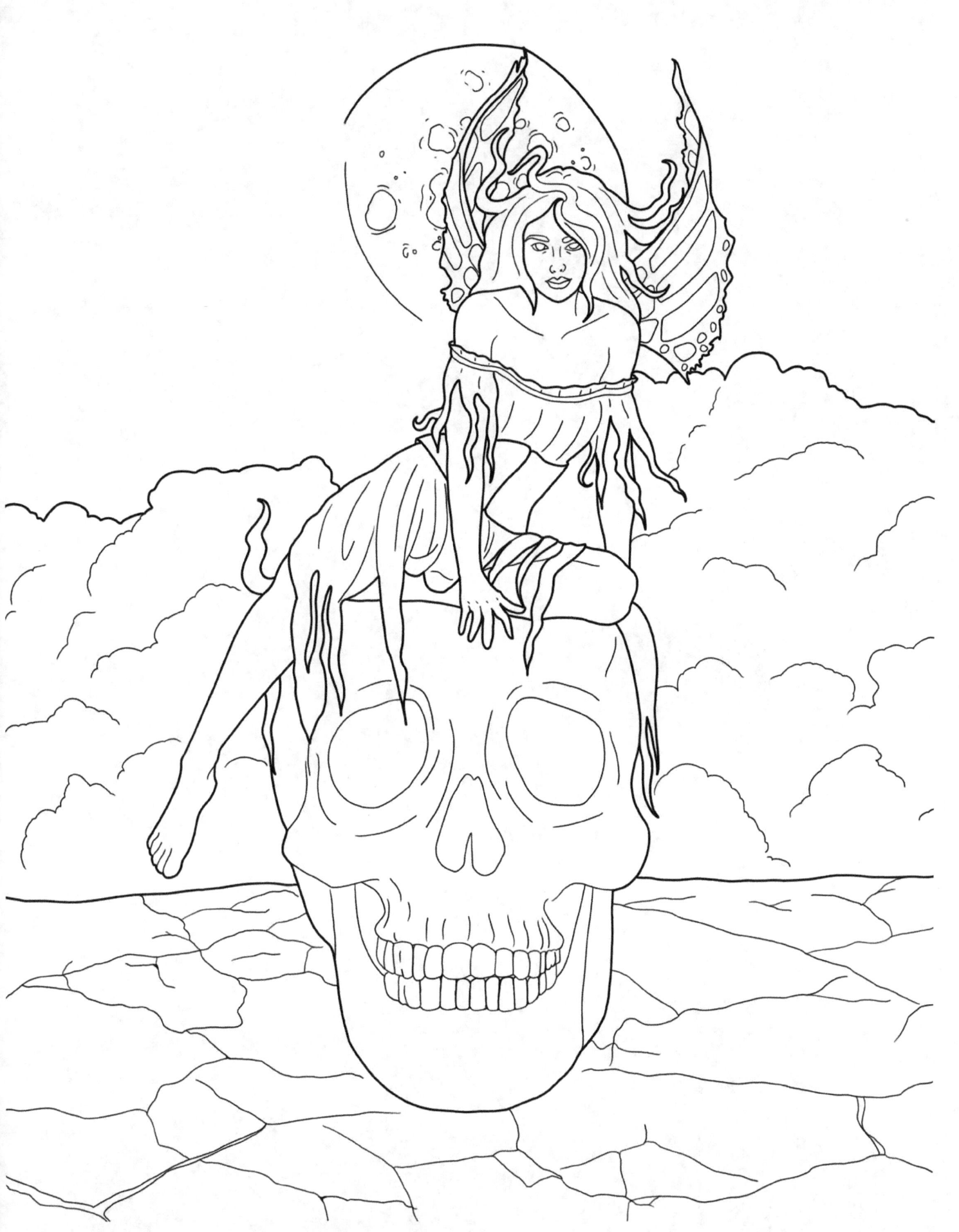

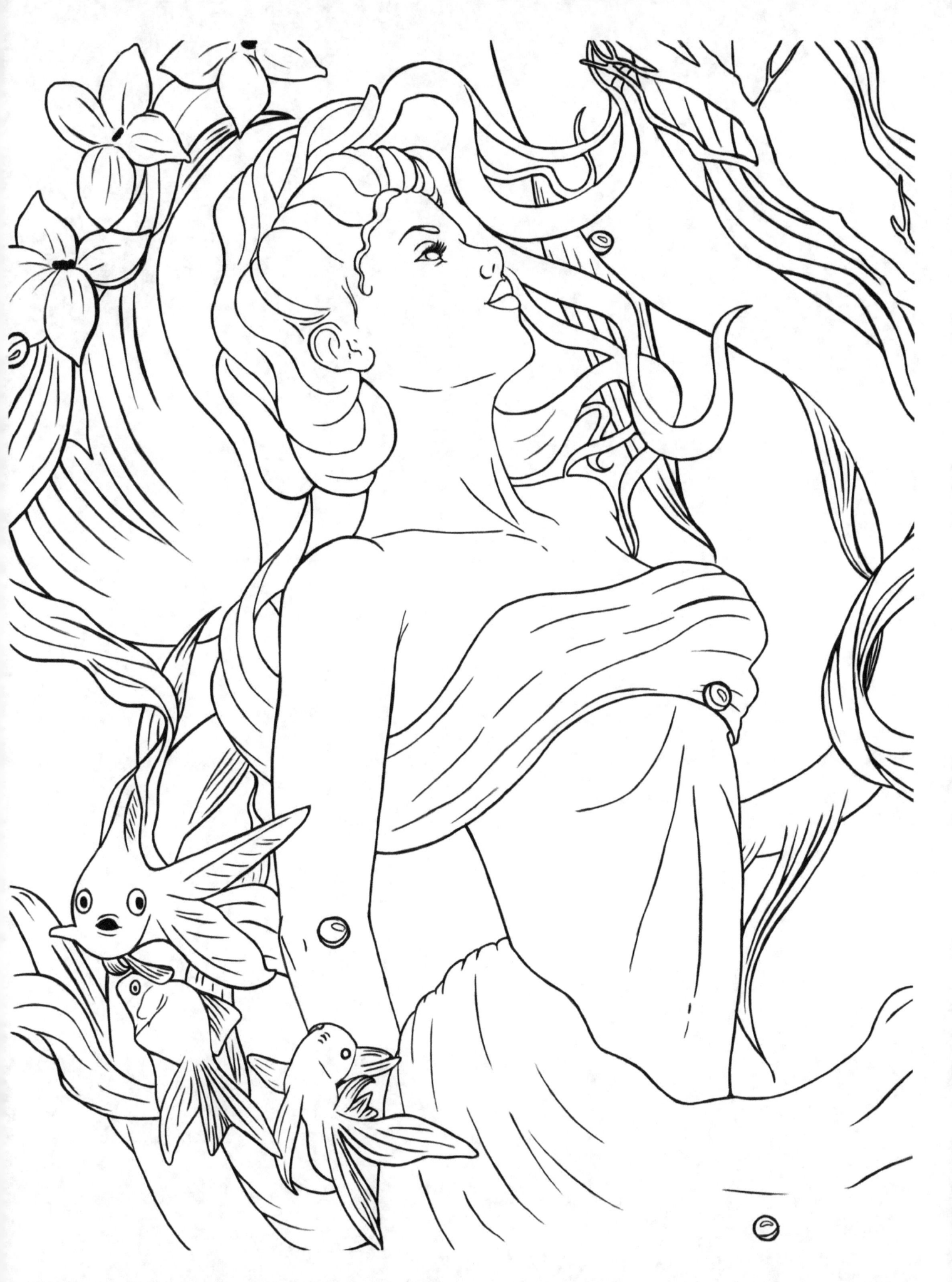

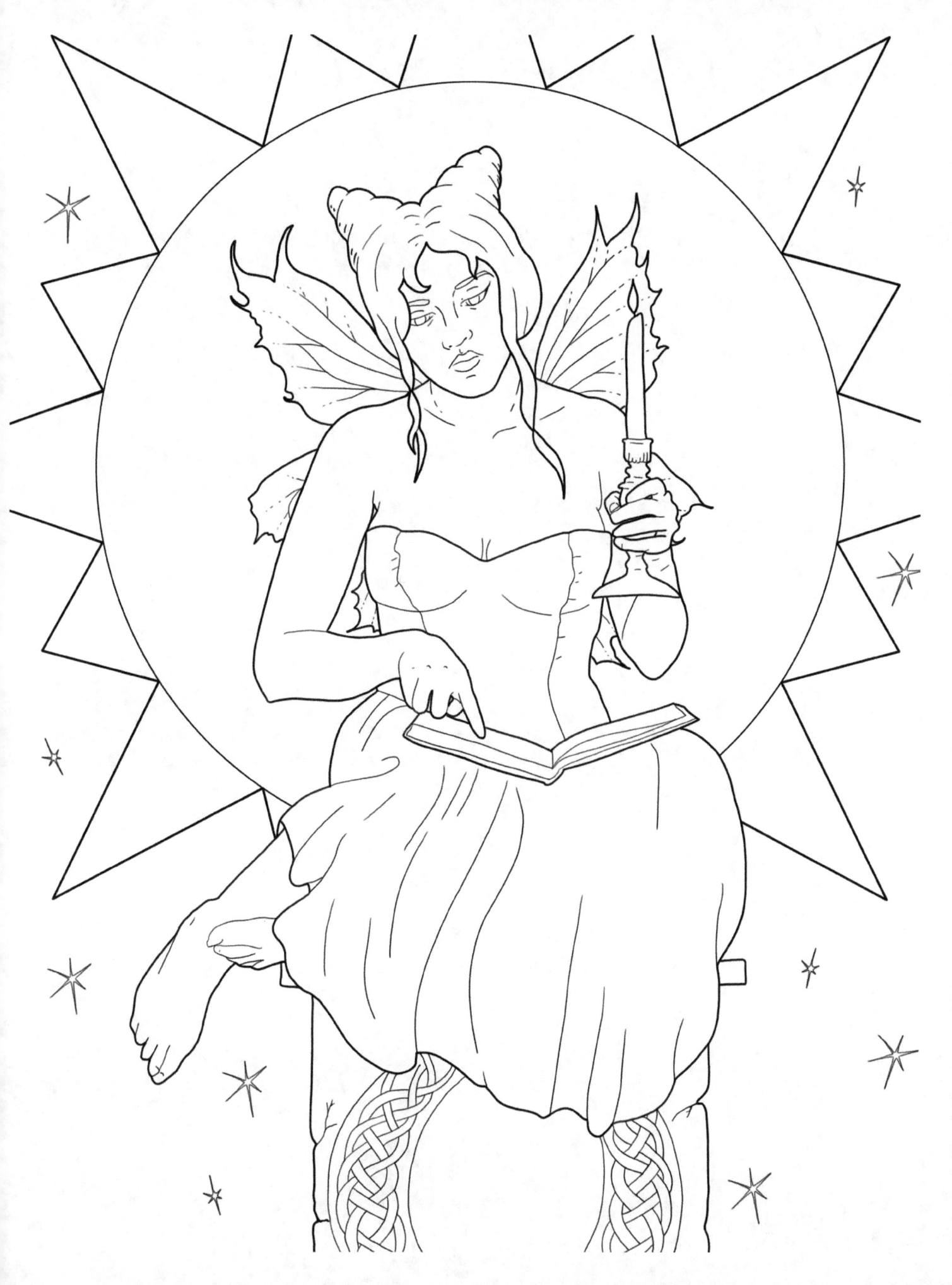

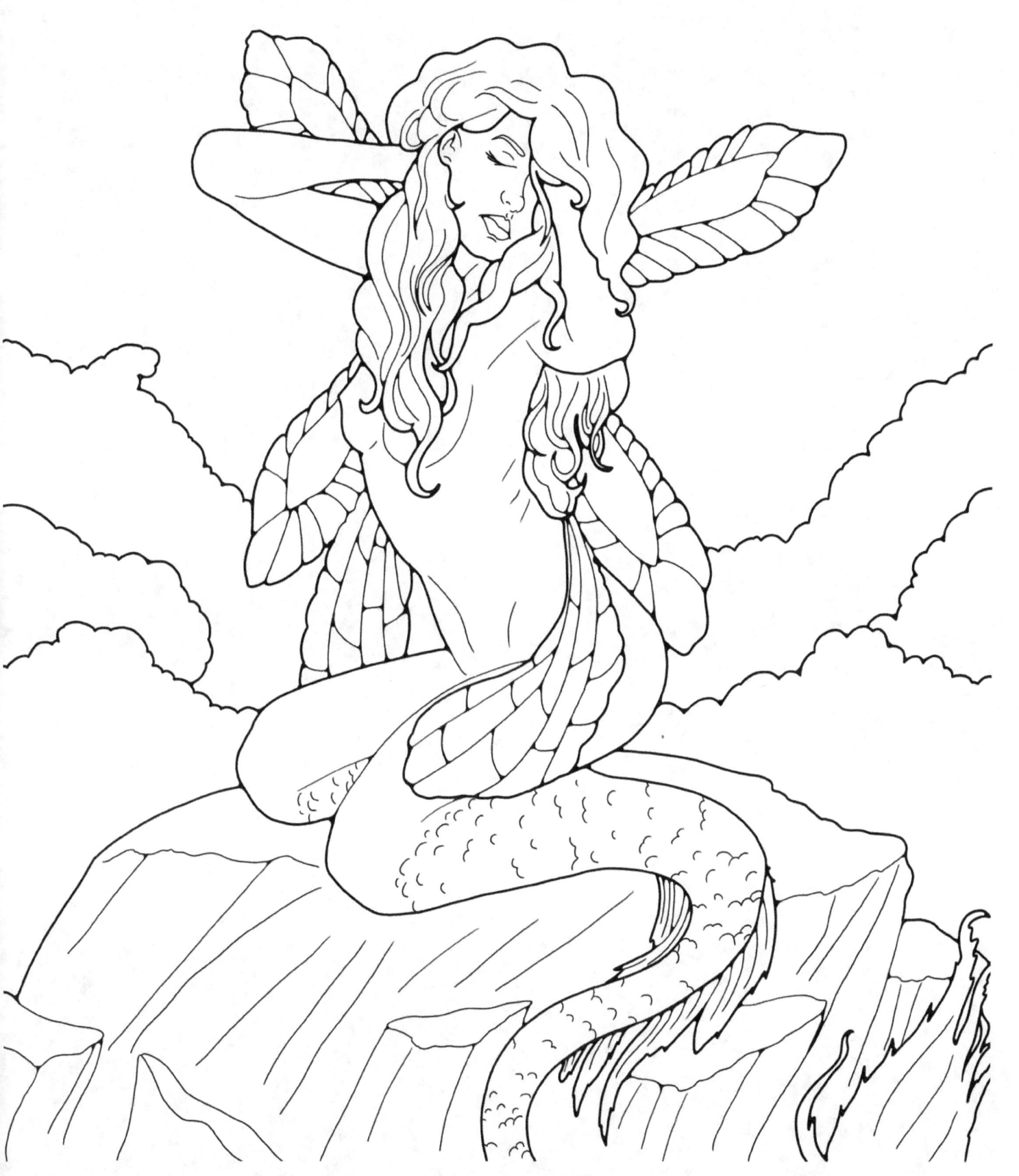

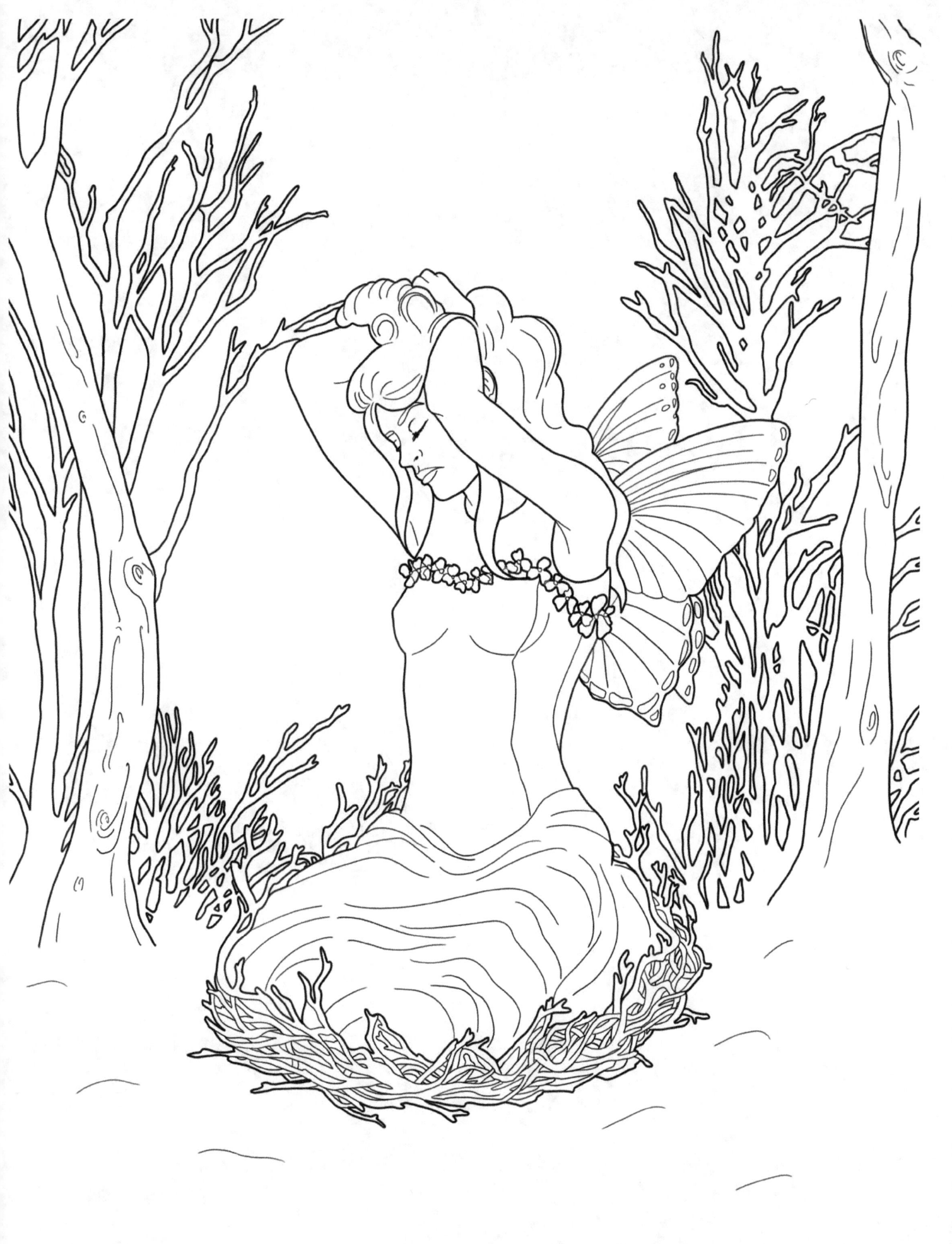

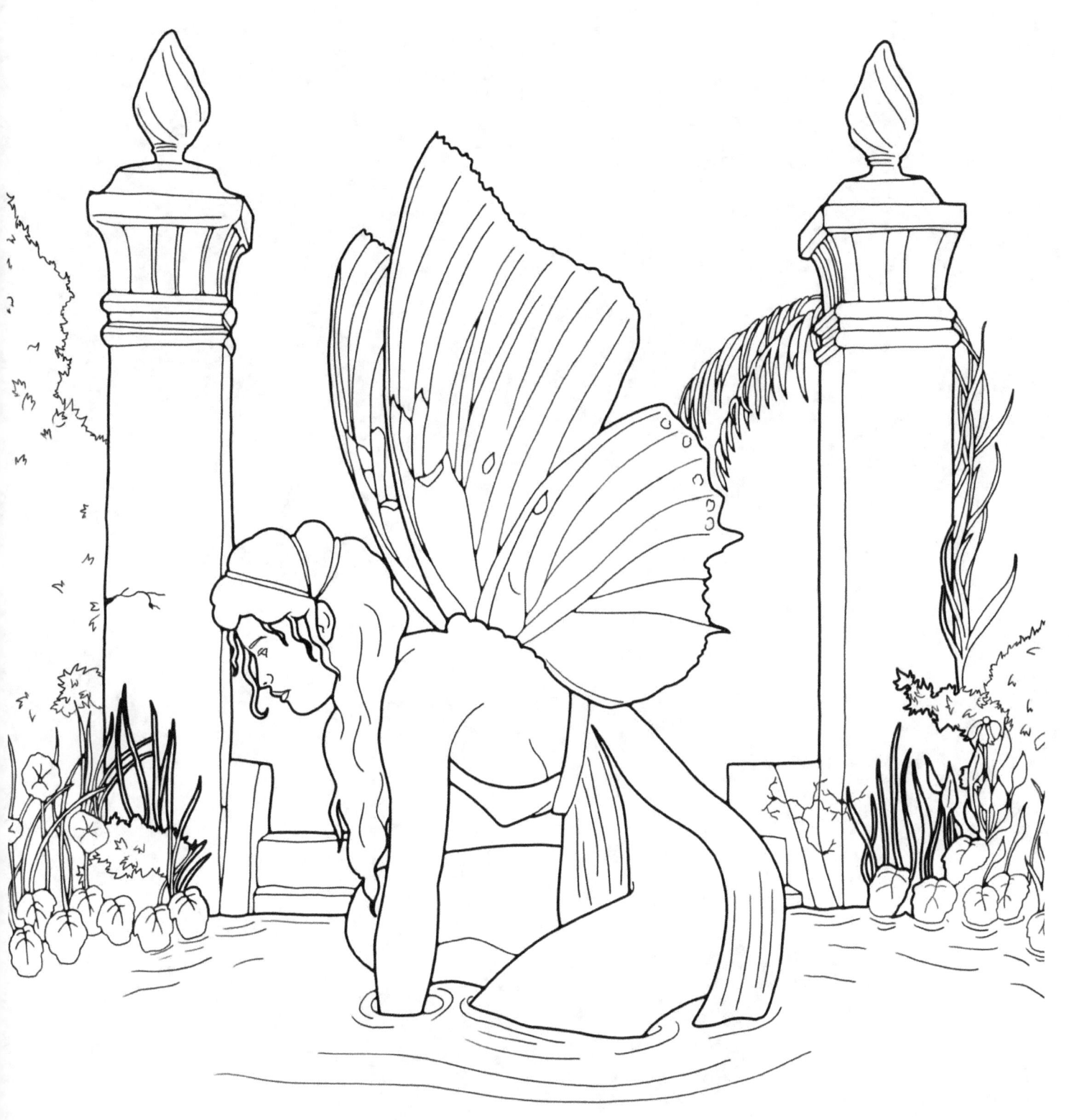

"PORTAL TO ATLANTIS"

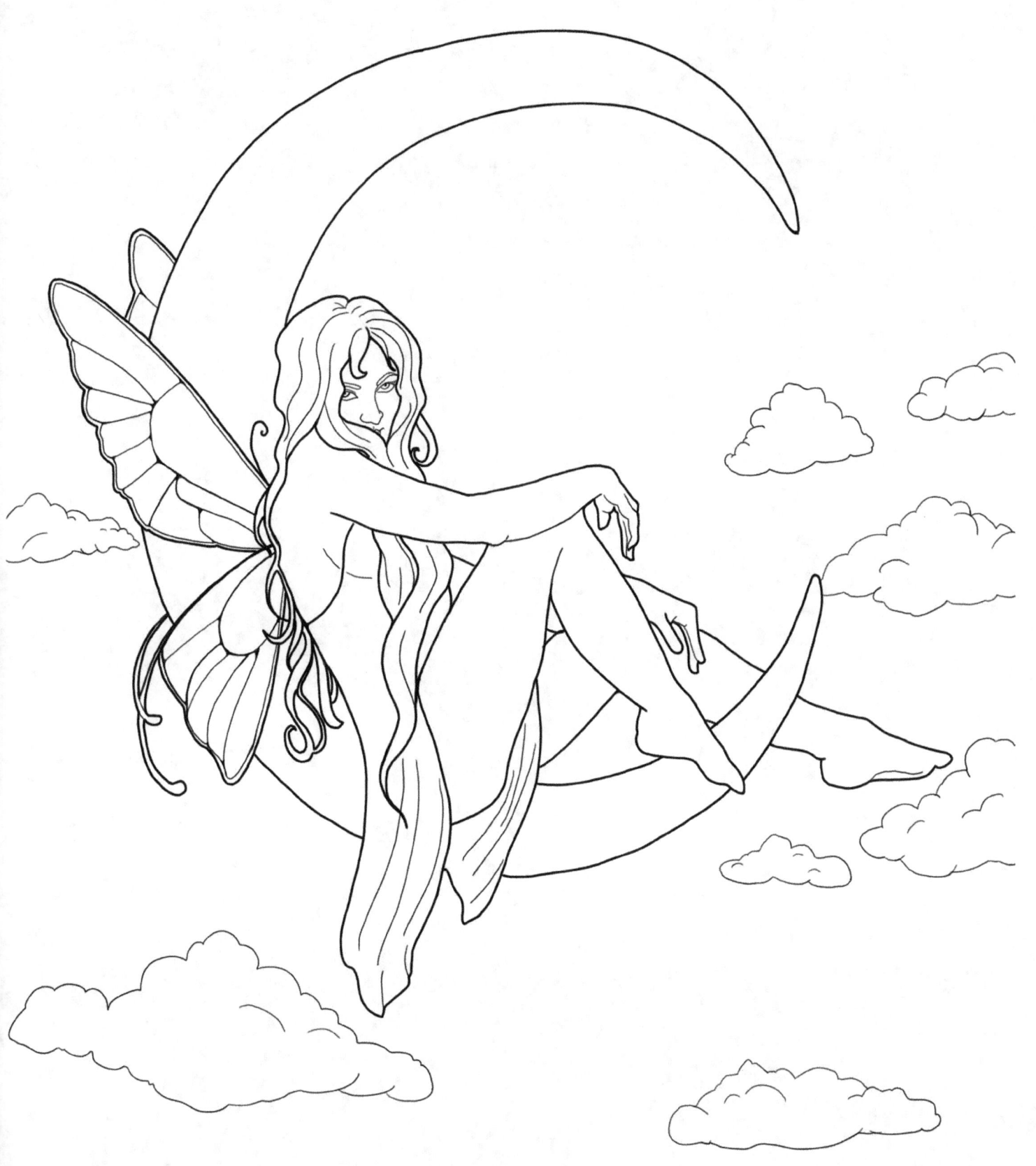

"WINTER MOON"

SPECIAL THANKS

To my husband, Luke, for taking care of everything while I worked
like a dog to finish this project,
my son, Wolfgang, for being a good boy so mommy could work,
and to everyone who supported this project via Kickstarter!

See more and keep up to date with new projects at

www.titoland.com

www.ingramcontent.com/pod-product-compliance
Lightning Source LLC
Chambersburg PA
CBHW080922170526
45158CB00008B/2199